IMPROVISATION IN THE MUSIC CLASSROOM

Sequential Learning

Also by Edwin E. Gordon:

A Music Learning Theory for Newborn and Young Children

Learning Sequences in Music

The Psychology of Music Teaching

Study Guide for Learning Sequences in Music

The Nature, Description, Measurement, and Evaluation of Music Aptitudes

Designing Objective Research in Music Education

The Musical Aptitude Profile

The Iowa Tests of Music Literacy

Primary Measures of Music Audiation

Intermediate Measures of Music Audiation

Advanced Measures of Music Audiation

Guiding Your Child's Music Development

Audie

Music Audiation Games

Rhythm: Contrasting the Implications of Audiation and Notation

Introduction to Research and the Psychology of Music

Preparatory Audiation, Audiation, and Music Learning Theory

Rating Scales and Their Uses for Measuring and Evaluating Achievement in Music Performance

IMPROVISATION IN THE MUSIC CLASSROOM

Sequential Learning

Edwin E. Gordon
*Author, Lecturer
and Researcher*

G-6180

GIA Publications, Inc.
Chicago

Improvisation in the Music Classroom
© Copyright 2003 GIA Publications, Inc.
7404 S. Mason Ave., Chicago, IL 60638 • www.giamusic.com
International copyright secured
Library of Congress Catalog Card Number: 97-21939
ISBN: 1-57999-221-8
Printed in U.S.A.

TABLE OF CONTENTS

Preface vii

Part One
    INTRODUCTION 1

Part Two
    THE NATURE OF IMPROVISATION 11

Part Three
    RHYTHM 15

Part Four
    TONALITIES 33

Part Five
    MELODIC PATTERNS 43

Part Six
    HARMONIC PATTERNS 63

Part Seven
    HARMONIC IMPROVISATION-A 65

Part Eight
    HARMONIC IMPROVISATION-B 85

Part Nine
    ADVANCED HARMONIC IMPROVISATION-A 93

Part Ten
    ADVANCED HARMONIC IMPROVISATION-B 105

Part Eleven
    ADVANCED HARMONIC IMPROVISATION-C 109

Part Twelve
    MAKING THE TRANSITION FROM VOICE TO INSTRUMENTS . .115

Glossary 120

Index 131

Preface

Customarily, improvisation is taught in jazz ensembles. My purpose for writing this book is unmistakable. It is to assist classroom teachers in teaching improvisation to students who are not enrolled in special music classes or in elective music activities. It is students in the general music classroom who are my interest.

It is important that all students enjoy experiences in improvisation. My reason for this opinion is that improvisation pervades all aspects of music, not only instrumental performance. When we interpret music notation and when we listen to music, each one of us participates with different ears depending upon our unique musical background and our music potential in terms of music aptitudes. The fact that we listen and read distinctively testifies that, apart from instrumental performance, we also engage in improvisation. As will be discovered, a student need not perform or sing in a jazz style to improvise. In fact, some of the most interesting improvisations are inchoate, and they may come forth at the most unexpected times and places by students of all ages. In a word, the more a student engages in improvisation, the better that student will learn to listen to music, read music notation, interpret music, and perform music expressively.

Do not be intimidated by improvisation. If you, yourself, do not purposefully improvise, you will quickly become captivated and assured as a result of learning along with the students you are teaching. The step-by-step approach outlined herein will facilitate your and your students' understanding and confidence. The material in the book establishes a firm foundation in improvisation. If you wish to go beyond the limits of this book, such as audiating and using added-sixth, major-seventh, ninth chords, and augmented-eleventh chords, you and your students will be well equipped to do so.

Two points that may be of ancillary interest follow. First, songs have not been included in the book because it has been my experience that students, even in the same classroom, no longer share a common or standard repertoire of folk songs. Thus, it will be up to you to identify or teach songs to your students if you wish to use them in improvisation. Second, to be realistic and engender integrity, the examples of improvisations notated on the following pages represent the actual incipient innovations of students of various ages in all stages of achievement. Only a few are without some modification. Also, the majority of chord progressions forming the bases for improvisation in part ten were initiated by students.

May I make a request? Please look through the entire book to get an overview of the material. Among other things, it will prepare you for sequential teaching. Moreover, there may be some suggestions toward the end that you might find to be useful at an earlier time.

Improvisation is rooted in the Latin *improvisus,* which translates to "not provided" or "not foreseen."

Part One
Introduction

Improvisation is the essence, the sum and substance, of music. This is so for a variety of reasons. Everyone who listens to music brings to the experience his or her own cultural background, shaped by the general environment each was exposed to throughout life. Moreover, individuals have unique backdrops of music achievement. Some have studied music seriously and others only casually. Add to this panorama the effect of music aptitude, the potential to develop skills in understanding and performing music. The interaction of the three sources makes it immediately obvious that it is impossible for any two persons to listen to the same piece of music in the same manner. Specifically, every time an individual listens to music, that person is improvising to the extent that his or her singular personality ordains. Incidentally, the same process applies to language.

Improvisation goes beyond listening. Think of reading music notation vocally or instrumentally. Because of its very nature, music notation is imprecise. In addition, the most important aspects of music cannot be translated into symbols on the printed page. Then there is the creative act that manifests itself in composition. Possibly with the exception of a genius like Mozart, the first attempt at writing a composition is not the composer's final outcome. Now consider the fact that no two conductors interpret a piece of music alike. Interpretation and improvisation go hand-in-hand. Further, many orchestral musicians will report that it is the rare conductor who is not improving at some time during a performance, always audiating better ways to elucidate a composition. Finally, reflect on the most current description of improvisation, for example, practiced by J. S. Bach and currently by jazz musicians. Improvisation of this type is the pinnacle of musicianship.

Suffice it to say that the more one is capable of improvisation, regardless of whether music is followed as a vocation or an avocation, the better that person will overall respond to music. Every human is capable of improvising to some extent. All that is required to impel this reality is appropriate guidance, guidance that emphasizes learning rather than teaching with special attention given to individual differences personified by the unique levels of music aptitudes each person possesses.

From an historical perspective of music education, improvisation has largely been ignored. Only in the past few years have improvisation classes begun to be offered at the college and university level, not usually in the general curriculum, but for those select students who pursue jazz studies. The same is true in the lower schools. The establishment directs that emphasis be placed on imitation and memorization in the performance of music created by established composers and arrangers. Thus, music notation and music theory on the one hand and instrumental and vocal technique on the other are the mainstays in the elementary, middle, and secondary schools. They receive primary attention in instructional programs. But without improvisation to serve as a foundation, at best only minimal achievement in other music endeavors may be anticipated. Nonetheless, for a diversity of dubious personal and pedagogical reasons, the crust of convention persists. Challenging tradition necessarily brings about change, and no one is dismayed by and resists change more than methodologists.

The word *audiation* and the term *music aptitudes* require explanation because of their importance in understanding the nature of improvisation and in guiding students in learning to improvise.

There are some other introductory concepts that need to be touched upon as well. Each will be discussed briefly before turning directly to improvisation in part two. For more detailed information about music aptitudes, however, see Edwin E. Gordon, *Introduction to Research and the Psychology of Music,* Chicago: GIA, 1998, and about audiation, preparatory audiation, and related precepts, see Edwin E. Gordon, *Preparatory Audiation, Audiation, and Music Learning Theory,* Chicago: GIA, 2001 and Edwin E. Gordon, *Learning Sequences in Music: Skill, Content, and Patterns,* Chicago: GIA, 2003.

Audiation

A simple definition of audiation is the capability of hearing **and understanding** music for which the sound is not or may never have been physically present. Although music is not a language, the process is the same for audiating and giving meaning to music as for thinking and giving meaning to speech. When you are listening to speech, you are giving meaning to what was just said by recalling and making connections with what you have heard on earlier occasions. At the same time, you are anticipating or predicting what you will be hearing next, based on your experience and understanding. Similarly, when you are listening to music, you are giving meaning to what you just heard by recalling what you have heard on earlier occasions. At the same time, you are anticipating or predicting what you will be hearing next, based on your music achievement. In other words, when you are audiating as you are listening to music, you are summarizing and generalizing from the specific music patterns you have just heard and are momentarily hearing as a way of anticipating or predicting what will follow. Every action becomes an interaction. What you are audiating depends on what you have already audiated. As audiation develops, the broader and deeper it becomes and thus the more it is able to reflect on itself.

We also audiate when we assimilate and comprehend in our minds music that we may or may not have heard but are reading in notation or are composing or improvising. Aural perception takes place when we are actually hearing sound the moment as it is being produced. We audiate actual sound only after we have aurally perceived it. In aural perception we are dealing with immediate sound events. In audiation, however, we are dealing with delayed musical events. Moreover, compared to what is often called musical imagery, audiation is a more profound process. Musical imagery simply suggests a vivid or figurative picture of what the sound of music might represent. It does not require the assimilation and comprehension of the musical sound itself, as does audiation.

Sound itself is not music. Sound becomes music only through audiation, when, as with language, you translate the sounds in your mind to give them meaning. The meaning you give to these sounds will be different on different occasions as well as different from that given them by any other person. As explained, you are improvising. Your level of music aptitude and the extent of your education and experience determines the quality of meaning you are able to offer to music at any given time.

It would be difficult, if not impossible, to describe all of the ways and combinations of ways in which musicians audiate. Consider, for example, the way drummers in a jazz ensemble audiate the melody of a song as they are improvising a solo and the intricate patterns of sound conductors are continually audiating as they are guiding a symphony orchestra. Consider also how differently performers audiate when they interpret a piece of music as a soloist from when they play in ensemble. Obviously it is more difficult for ensemble players to audiate what their colleagues are performing than it is for them to audiate their own part. Whether elementary or advanced, vocal or instrumental, solo or ensemble, however, audiation is a matter of concentrating on one set of musical sounds while at the same time attending to or performing one or more sets of other musical sounds. When they are practicing and not audiating, musicians are conscious of what they are doing and they absorb the music. When they are performing and audiating, however, musicians are unconscious of what they are doing and the music absorbs them. Fine musicians know when they are audiating: it is when the ears become more important than the fingers.

Some musicians are capable of audiating one piece of music while they are listening to or performing another, and other musicians are capable of audiating the inner and lower parts of a piece of music while they are audiating its melody. Musicians who are truly improvising may be audiating aspects of a piece of music they are performing that are different from what is actually being performed, the chord progression in jazz, for example, that underlies the melody or the melody that underlies a variation. A jazz instrumentalist, scat singer, or rap performer may audiate a phrase from one piece of music and substitute it for the original phrase in the piece of music he or she is performing. Scat singers and rap performers, like some instrumentalists, may not even be able to explain in technical or theoretical terms what they are audiating. Whereas most musicians who perform jazz through imitation can perform in only one style, those who audiate can comfortably improvise jazz in two or more styles, such as both swing and bop. Composers who audiate, those who are not dependent on an instrument while composing, usually audiate several aspects of the music they are creating concurrently, such as the melody, harmony, phrasing, and instrumentation. Such composers audiate in silence, just as artists "see in the dark." All capable musicians anticipate and predict in audiation what they expect to hear, perform, improvise, or create before they actually engage in listening, performing, improvising, or composing.

Like imitation, memory and recognition are part of the audiation process. Alone, however, they are not audiation. We can recognize a piece of music, even music performed with some incorrect pitches and durations, and still not be able to audiate it. We might be aware only of its melodic contour and rhythm. Many persons who recognize *Happy Birthday* are unable to sing its resting tone, to identify and move to its fundamental beats, to hear its tonality and meter, or to specify the chord progression that underlies its melody.

Most students and probably most musicians memorize a piece of music without being able to audiate it contextually. Memorizing music on an instrument is primarily related to fingerings and other technical matters and not to the audiation of the music itself. How many persons do you know who can play a melody on an instrument but are unable to sing what they have played; to play a variation of the original melody; to play the melody in a different keyality, tonality, or with alternate fingerings; or to demonstrate with body movement the phrases of the melody? To the extent that they cannot do these things, they are not audiating what they have performed. It is as if they were reciting words they had memorized without ascribing meaning to them.

Music Aptitudes

Music aptitude is a measure of a student's potential to learn music. It points beyond itself. Music achievement is a measure of what a student has already learned in music. For example, a student is not born knowing how to improvise music in a given style. That must be learned, and once learned, is considered music achievement. Conversely, a student is born with more or less potential or capacity to learn to improvise music in a given style, and that potential is associated with at least two of the more than a dozen or so dimensions of music aptitude. It may help to understand this concept by distinguishing between the brain and the mind. Children are born with a brain. It is physically innate. As the brain becomes acculturated by the environment through the senses, the mind begins to be gradually acquired psychologically.

Different levels of music aptitudes require different approaches to teaching music. All students, regardless of their individual levels of music aptitudes can learn to improvise, and it is the teacher's professional responsibility to support every student in learning to improvise to the extent his or her potential will allow. Teaching to students' individual musical differences is requisite if all students are to learn to improvise. As will be explained throughout the book, given appropriate guidance, this can be accomplished easily in classroom music without making students with higher aptitudes vain or students with lower aptitudes insecure or embarrassed. Private lessons are neither recommended nor necessary. In general, once readiness has been provided, students gain more by listening to peers improvise in group activities than by being directed by a teacher.

Though it may be scorned by demagogues wedded to political correctness, an opinion stated more than a century ago by Felix Emanuel Schelling, an American educator and scholar, whose dates are 1858-1945, is apropos:

> True education makes for inequality; the inequality of individuality; the inequality of success; the glorious inequality of talent, of genius; for inequality, not mediocrity, individual superiority, not standardization, is the measure of the progress of this world.

Although a child is born with a particular level of music aptitude, that level changes in accordance with the quality of the child's informal and formal music environment until the child is about nine, and until that age, music aptitude is considered developmental. Thus, neither nature nor nurture is solely responsible for the child's level of music aptitude. Music aptitude is a product of both innate potential and environmental influences. Regardless of the quality of students' music environment after age nine, however, it will no longer have any effect on their levels of music aptitude. Music aptitude becomes stabilized. That is, a student's potential to achieve in music remains throughout life what it was at nine years old. For example, the level of students' potential to learn to improvise is commensurate with their levels of stabilized music aptitude. Be clear: Even though the upper limit of music achievement is bound by stabilized levels of music aptitudes, and students' music aptitudes become stabilized at around age nine, students can certainly achieve in music after age nine through adulthood. It is said that most persons use approximately only ten-percent of their potential to achieve. Thus, regardless of how low a student's music aptitudes may be, he or she may still achieve ninety-percent more than is currently demonstrated. The importance of parents and teachers providing appropriate early childhood music experiences for newborn and young children, however, cannot be overestimated. Relevant information may be found in Edwin E. Gordon, *A Music Learning Theory for Newborn and Young Children*, Chicago: GIA, 2003.

Readiness, Teaching, and Sequential Learning

Learning is most appropriate when it is sequential. Sequential learning takes place when a teacher determines what a student needs to know in order to learn what is being taught. Without proper readiness, learning becomes fragmented, and thus, students find it arduous to meet their own or the expectations of the teacher. Readiness, of course, is presupposed and assured when learning is sequential.

The most important things in life cannot be taught, they can only be learned. Teachers can only guide students as students are participating in the learning process. Teaching takes place outside the student, whereas learning takes place inside the student. Specifically, improvisation cannot be taught, the student must learn to improvise. That is accomplished by a teacher preparing the student to learn, in other words, assisting the student in acquiring the necessary readiness to learn to improvise. As with language, a child can be taught to repeat words, but it is not possible to teach the child to think and improvise a spoken phrase or sentence that conveys overall intelligent meaning using those words. Familiarity with environmental conditions and the acquisition of words is the readiness for asking and answering questions, just as the audiation of musical context and content is the readiness for engaging in improvisation. It should be apparent that improvisation occurs not only in language and music, but as a matter of fact, in every aspect of human cognition, bar none.

Content and Context

As a parallel to music, think again of language. Individual words represent content. After words are connected into sentences and phrases, contextual meaning is generated. That is, when words are put together, collectively they tell a story. Similarly, there are tonal, rhythm, melodic, harmonic, and temporal patterns in music. They are the "words" of music, and individually they are referred to as the content of a piece of music. After these patterns are strung together and a tonality (such as major, minor, Dorian, and so on) emerges and a meter (such as duple, triple, and so on) emerges, that constitutes a sentence or phrase in music. Tonalities and meters, regardless of whether they are audiated objectively (with consensus) or subjectively (without consensus), are referred to as the context of a piece of music. To be taught content before being exposed to the foundation that context provides introduces many debilitating problems that seriously impede learning music, particularly learning to improvise. The principle of context before content in learning to improvise will loom large in further discussions.

Research

The substance of this book is based on the results of observational and experimental research. Procedures in the teaching/learning improvisation process have been examined and appropriate musical content and context for best providing sequential learning for students possessing differential levels of music aptitudes have been established. Moreover, the substance of the majority of the notated examples of developmental improvisations were transcribed from students' actual performances in the classroom. Descriptions of the designs of the research studies and accompanying results can be found in Edwin E. Gordon, *Studies in Harmonic and Rhythmic Improvisation*, Chicago: GIA, 2000. Valid tests for measuring and evaluating singly or in groups individual students' readiness to begin improvisational activities in music are available. For information about relevant tests and prepublication research, see Edwin E. Gordon, *Harmonic Improvisation Readiness Record and Rhythm Improvisation Readiness Record,* Chicago: GIA, 1998.

Part Two
The Nature of Improvisation

Whether contemplating the enjoyment of simply listening to music or the pedagogy of music education, the concepts of audiation, music aptitude, and improvisation must be considered as a whole. Audiation (as explained, the hearing and understanding of music for which the sound is not or may have never been physically present) is the basis of music aptitude. Music aptitude (as explained, an indication of the degree of potential for learning music) is fundamental to music achievement, which includes, of course, the improvisation of music. Improvisation is not to be confused with creativity. Though they share a continuum, creativity is prepared composition whereas improvisation is spontaneous composition. It is reasonable to believe, nonetheless, that "chance" favors the prepared mind.

More and more, music educators and the public at large are realizing the role and value of improvisation in the enjoyment and understanding of music, particularly in terms of listening to and participating in the making of music. Without audiation as the source, at most, music can elicit only emotional response, much like eating and not digesting food. More specifically, audiation expressed through improvisation (musical conversation) best precedes being taught to read the notation of music, because improvisation appropriately becomes the readiness for learning to read music notation just as language conversation becomes the readiness for learning to read the printed symbols that represent a language.

There are many pedagogical approaches for teaching (explaining to another) music improvisation, but the question of how one learns (explaining to oneself) to improvise in terms of a music learning theory has received relatively little attention. As alluded to, that begs the question of whether improvisation can actually be taught. In other words, only the readiness to learn to improvise can be taught, and improvisation, itself, has to be learned. Just as a vocabulary of words, not thinking, can be taught, all a teacher can do is provide students with the necessary readiness to teach themselves how to improvise. That readiness consists of acquiring a vocabulary of tonal patterns, rhythm patterns, melodic patterns (the combining of tonal and rhythm patterns), and harmonic patterns as they relate to temporal aspects in music.

Improvisation may take place in three ways. First, one may perform a variation of a melody without giving attention to the underlying existent or implied harmony. Often, particularly with musically immature instrumentalists performing in a jazz style, their melodic improvisation is guided by chord symbols, although they are not able to audiate the harmony that the symbols represent. For example, when reading and playing in C and a G7 chord symbol is seen, they are instructed to perform fragments of or an entire Mixolydian scale, but they usually are not aware aurally of the relation of that chord to the tonic of the keyality or to the resting tone of the tonality of the music. They tend to repeat what others play, if not what they, themselves, have played only moments ago. They quote themselves over and over again. Second, musicians may perform a melody over a series of harmonic patterns, otherwise called harmonic pattern progressions. In the vernacular, they are referred to simply as "the changes." The harmonic patterns, themselves, provide the basis for the improvisation, and the improvisation may or may not be a variation of an established melody. It is much like the way it was done when musicians improvised from a figured bass during the Baroque. Persons who "sing in harmony" by improvising a second part are, of course, also aware of the underlying harmonic patterns. Third, musicians may improvise harmonic patterns to an old or new melody.

The first method requires memorization and imitation. Knowledge of music theory and knowing how to read music notation are helpful, if not necessary. The second and third methods require audiation. It is because what audiation is to music, thought is to language, I believe improvisation, if it is to be worthwhile, is best learned by engaging in the second and third methods. I must emphasize, however, that the vertical structure of chords, that is, the position of individual pitches within chords, is irrelevant to the context of harmonic patterns. When chords are taught as independent vertical functions, the emphasis is on theory and rules of part-writing. When chords are taught in linear fashion, as collectively constituting one or more harmonic patterns, the emphasis is on musical context.

Part Three
Rhythm

Improvisation best begins with rhythm improvisation. Rhythm improvisation is basic because it provides the readiness for sequentially learning the higher orders of improvisation. Next in the hierarchy comes tonal improvisation, then melodic improvisation (combining rhythm and tonal improvisation), and harmonic improvisation is the culmination. After the component parts of rhythm are described and notated below, rhythm patterns will be presented, and finally rhythm improvisation will be addressed.

You probably will discover that the following explanations about rhythm are different from what you have been taught, what you are being taught, or what you might be teaching. Granting that the nature and organization of rhythm can never adequately be explained to everyone's satisfaction, it has been my experience that when rhythm is presented to students in accord with the following explanations, they quickly will learn to improvise rhythmically, and especially with understanding and confidence.

Definition of Rhythm

The three universal elements of rhythm are macrobeats, microbeats, and rhythm patterns. Rhythm patterns establish the rhythm of the melody or the rhythm of the text; microbeats establish meter and form the basis of rhythmic context; and macrobeats establish tempo. In audiation, rhythm patterns are superimposed on microbeats, and microbeats are superimposed on macrobeats. It is most important to realize that all three elements must be audiated concurrently, as if they are all functioning in circular space to establish rhythmic context. When one element is missing in audiation, rhythm, for all intents and purposes, becomes rigid. As a consequence, among other things, the rhythm of a piece of music becomes erratic, because durations haphazardly become longer and shorter than they should be, entrances after rests are early and late, meter changes without purpose, and consistency of tempo is compromised.

Rhythm patterns, though not fundamental, are the most obvious of the three elements of rhythm. Unfortunately, many persons presume that what is commonly thought of as rhythm — that is, ongoing series of rhythm patterns in time — is all there is to rhythm. There is much more to rhythm than that. As explained, think of meter as the context and rhythm patterns as the content of a piece of music, with macrobeats providing the substructure for both.

Below is an explanation of macrobeats, microbeats, and rhythm patterns as they function in the three usual meters. There are also four unusual meters, but too satisfy the immediate purposes of this book, they are not considered herein. For more detailed information about rhythm, explanations and the improvisation of unusual meters, and multimetric and multitemporal music, see Edwin E. Gordon, *Rhythm: Contrasting the Implications of Audiation and Notation*, Chicago: GIA, 2000.

Macrobeats

Sing or chant the beginning of a march. Move to and feel the longest beats of equal duration, perhaps those that you might march to as you are singing and chanting. While not all persons will identify the same beats as the longest, whichever beats you feel to be longest are called macrobeats. Notice that although you are accenting and pairing macrobeats in audiation, you are pairing but probably are not always accenting all macrobeats, especially the first of the pair, as you perform them. Obviously, to perform all macrobeats with accents in the same way you audiate them would be to violate your own sense of artistic interpretation and expression. That is, it is natural in audiation to accent macrobeats that in performance would be rendered in a more fluid fashion. Imagine a clock as you are accenting macrobeats in audiation. Imagine an hour glass as you are freely moving to macrobeats in performance.

As stated previously, macrobeats, microbeats, and rhythm patterns are the universal elements of rhythm. Macrobeats are fundamental to our feeling of the microbeats and rhythm patterns in music, because microbeats and rhythm patterns are superimposed in audiation on macrobeats. Presented below are notational examples of macrobeats in usual meter using a variety of arbitrarily chosen measure signatures. Notice that quarter notes do not always represent macrobeats. For example, in 3/4, it is dotted-half notes, not quarter notes, that are the macrobeats. The same rhythm pattern can, of course, be notated using a variety of measure signatures, and the same measure signature can be used to notate rhythm patterns in a variety of meters. To that extent, just as there are enharmonic key signatures and tonal patterns, there are enrhythmic measure signatures and rhythm patterns.

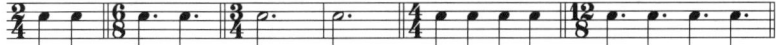

Microbeats and Meters

Microbeats are shorter than macrobeats and they are derived from the equal division of macrobeats. When macrobeats are divided into two microbeats of equal length (the first of the two coinciding with a macrobeat), usual duple meter is the result. When macrobeats are divided into three microbeats of equal length (the first of the three microbeats coinciding with a macrobeat), usual triple meter is the result. When some macrobeats are divided into two microbeats of equal length and other macrobeats are divided into three microbeats of equal length, each of the three microbeats being shorter than each of the two microbeats, (the first of the two or three microbeats coinciding with a macrobeat), usual combined meter is the result. The sequence of the groupings of twos or threes has no effect on the meter. In usual combined meter, then, all macrobeats are of equal length, but not all microbeats are of equal length. As compared to unusual meter, when macrobeats are audiated in pairs and are of equal length, the music is considered to be in usual meter.

Presented below are notational examples of microbeats in usual duple meter, usual triple meter, and usual combined meter using a variety of arbitrarily chosen measure signatures. So that the pairing of macrobeats can be seen in one measure, usual triple meter is notated in 6/8, with dotted-quarter notes being the macrobeats and eighth notes being the microbeats. Usual triple meter could have just as easily been notated in 3/4, for example, with dotted-half notes being the macrobeats and quarter notes being the microbeats.

There is no direct relation between notation, particularly a measure signature, and the meter of a piece of music. Though you may have been taught, for example, that the measure signature 6/8 indicates duple compound meter, that is inaccurate. In 6/8, two macrobeats (dotted-quarter notes) are audiated in each measure, and each macrobeat is divided into three microbeats (eighth notes). Specifically, the type of usual meter of a piece of music is not determined by how notes are grouped in a measure, but by how macrobeats are audiated and divided into microbeats — regardless of the measure signature. Thus, to avoid confusion, do not think about and rely on what you have been taught about rhythm notation. Only after you audiate and absorb the information here should you make comparisons between what you have been and are being taught, or between what you are teaching and what you are currently learning. Meanwhile, as you continue to read, please keep the following in mind:

1. The speed of macrobeats has no systematic effect on meter. Nevertheless, because macrobeats that are further apart seem to make meter and rhythm patterns more difficult to audiate, particularly for persons with low rhythm aptitude, macrobeats that are closer together assist in more quickly and accurately recognizing or identifying meter in a piece of music. Moreover, though our sense of the placement of macrobeats in a piece of music may initially be subjective, when it becomes objective, so will the meter of the music become objective. Our initial placement of macrobeats is akin to speculation which is confirmed (or denied) as we further experience the music.

2. Accents do not produce meter. They help only in establishing meter in audiation. Consider a waltz. There is, for example, an American waltz, a French waltz, a German waltz, and a Russian waltz. In all four types, every macrobeat (each of which occurs at the same time as the first of the three microbeats in each grouping) is accented in audiation. Whether there are macrobeats and microbeats that are accented in performance is a matter of cultural or ethnic tradition. Nonetheless, regardless of which beats are accented in a particular interpretation, all interpretations are true to usual triple meter.

3. The divisions of a microbeat have no effect on meter. If they did, music that is considered to be in usual duple meter would have to be reconsidered to be in usual triple meter if each of the duple microbeats (for example, eighth notes in 2/4) were further

divided into sixteenth-note triplets. Similarly, music that is considered to be in usual triple meter would have to be reconsidered to be in usual duple meter if each of the triple microbeats (for example, eighth notes in 6/8) were further divided into sixteenth notes.

4. Regardless of whether they are superimposed on an underlying macrobeat, microbeat, a division of a microbeat, or a division of a division of a microbeat, four durations in a grouping seems to be the limit of our audiation abilities.

5. Just as we must be audiating an underlying resting tone in order to give tonal context to music, so we must continuously be audiating underlying macrobeats and microbeats to give rhythmic context to music.

Rhythm Patterns

Typically, a rhythm pattern in usual meter is not shorter than the length of one underlying macrobeat and is no longer than the length of two underlying macrobeats. A rhythm pattern, in addition to rests, ties, and upbeats, may include macrobeats, microbeats, as well as divisions and elongations of macrobeats and microbeats. Moreover, a single duration superimposed on two or more underlying macrobeats (a half note in 2/4, for example) is considered a rhythm pattern because the underlying macrobeats, themselves, are being audiated. The rhythm of a song (the rhythm of the melody or the lyric) consists of a series of rhythm patterns. By concurrently audiating the macrobeats and microbeats that underlie the series of rhythm patterns in a piece of music, we can confidently determine the meter of that music. Every series of rhythm patterns (not necessarily individual rhythm patterns) is unique to one meter.

Remember, macrobeats are foundational to microbeats, and microbeats underlie a series of rhythm patterns. Stated in reverse, one could say that rhythm patterns are superimposed on microbeats, and microbeats are superimposed on macrobeats. When audiated concurrently, macrobeats, microbeats, and rhythm patterns lose their individual qualities and interact in a unique holistic manner — all three becoming one. Presented below are notational examples of two-pattern series of rhythm patterns in usual duple meter, usual triple meter, and usual combined meter, all notated with arbitrarily chosen measure signatures.

Presented below in score form in arbitrarily chosen measure signatures are notational examples of underlying macrobeats, underlying microbeats, and two-pattern series of rhythm patterns in the three usual meters: usual duple, usual triple, and usual combined.

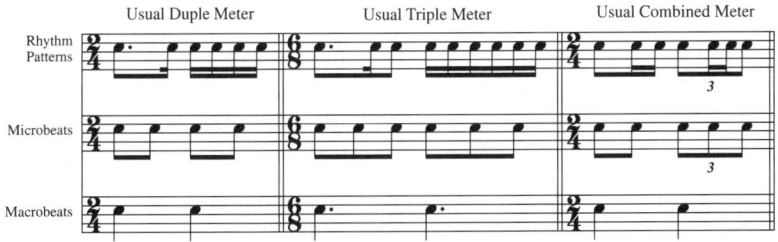

Rhythm Syllables

When rhythm patterns are audiated using rhythm syllables, students have a basis for quickly organizing and calling to mind appropriate rhythm patterns with specificity and clarity. Thus, the syllables can be used to recall efficiently rhythm patterns for purposes of improvisation, and teachers and students can interact more effectively by using an objective common language.

There are several systems of rhythm syllables. A few are intended strictly for purposes of instrumental articulation, others for learning to read music notation, and others for learning to audiate. The system described below is designed primarily to develop audiation skills, but it also serves well for acquiring notational audiation, that is, for comprehending what is seen in notation by audiating the symbols rather than by meaninglessly attempting to decode them. Traditionally, syllable names have been based on note values. The rhythm syllables presented below for the three usual meters are more logically and musically based on audible and silent (as in rests) macrobeats, microbeats, and their divisions and elongations.

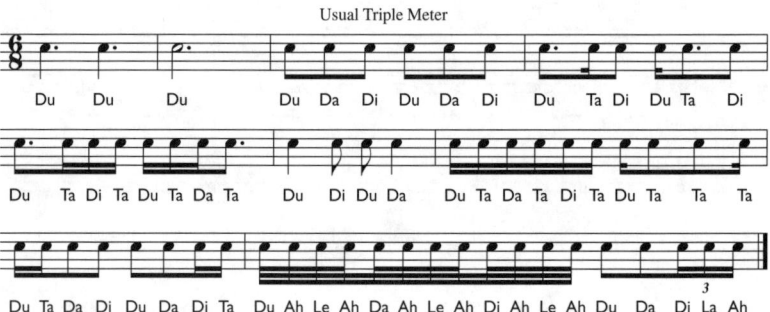

Rhythm Improvisation

The recommended sequential way to expose students to rhythm improvisation is described below by step for usual duple meter. These steps should be completed and reviewed over many class periods. For example, the first step may be introduced during one class period, the second step during the next class period, and so on. Review takes place as needed.

Before establishing context in any meter, model continuous flowing movement for the students. Begin with arms and hands and the upper part of the body standing in place. Next, the hips and legs are moved rather than the upper part of the body. Then the entire body is engaged. It is important that movement is free and comfortable, always continuous, covering as much self-space as possible. As students are moving in a continuous flowing manner, model the flicking of wrists to macrobeats, and then students imitate that action. After a complete stop, a new tempo is established. Finally, as movement remains continuous and flowing, the teacher and students move around the room at various tempi as they flick their wrists to macrobeats. Shoes might be removed and stocking-feet slid across the floor to insure that macrobeats are performed only with the wrists. When students show little or no evidence of rigidity, progress to the remaining sequential steps for each meter.

Section A - Usual Duple Meter

1. Perform one or more chants in usual duple meter, using **neutral syllables** (primarily *bah*), that incorporate repetition, sequence, and silence (rests). Students may or may not, as they wish, perform the chants. Encouraging students to listen and to audiate a specific meter before they perform, however, is essential. An example of a suitable chant in usual duple meter that you may perform for this purpose is notated below.

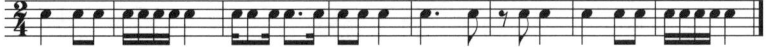

2. Maintaining a consistent tempo, all students move in a comfortable flowing manner to macrobeats. Discourage toe-tapping and encourage, if necessary, bouncing on heels. Next, all students move to microbeats. Then one group of students moves to macrobeats and another moves to microbeats. Reverse the groups. Do not use music as background to movement. Be alert that the tempo does not rush or slow. If it does, suggest that students use more space as they move their arms and legs, and that they move their hips from side-to-side rather than moving only their legs and feet.

3. Students *imitate* the teacher by chanting rhythm patterns with four underlying macrobeats using **neutral syllables** (primarily *bah*) as they are moving in a comfortable flowing manner to macrobeats and microbeats. Next, students *imitate* the teacher by chanting the rhythm patterns using rhythm syllables (*du* and *du-de*) as they continue to move to macrobeats and microbeats. Examples of rhythm patterns in usual duple meter are presented below.

4. Individual students, using **neutral syllables**, take turns **improvising** rhythm patterns as the class continues to move and chant macrobeats and microbeats. The patterns, including only **macrobeats and microbeats**, should be no longer or shorter than **four** underlying macrobeats. Next, individual students, using **rhythm syllables** (*du* and *du-de*), take turns *improvising* the rhythm patterns as the class continues to move and chant macrobeats and microbeats. Examples of what may be expected

of students' rhythm pattern improvisations are notated below in usual duple meter.

5. Individual students, using **neutral syllables**, take turns *improvising* rhythm patterns as the class continues to move and chant macrobeats and microbeats. The patterns, now expanded to include **macrobeats, microbeats, divisions, elongations, and/or rests** should be no longer or shorter than **four** underlying macrobeats. Next, individual students, using **rhythm syllables** (*du* and *du-de* and ta), take turns *improvising* the rhythm patterns as the class continues to move and chant macrobeats and microbeats. Examples of what may be expected of students' rhythm pattern improvisations are notated below in usual duple meter.

6. Individual students, using **neutral syllables**, take turns *improvising* rhythm patterns as the class continues to move and chant macrobeats and microbeats. The patterns, including **macrobeats, microbeats, divisions, elongations, and/or rests** are now no longer or shorter than **eight** underlying macrobeats. Next, individual students, using **rhythm syllables** (*du* and *du-de* and *ta*), take turns *improvising* the rhythm patterns as the class continues to move and chant macrobeats and microbeats.

Examples of what may be expected of students' rhythm pattern improvisations are notated below in usual duple meter.

Section B - Usual Triple Meter

1. Perform one or more chants in usual triple meter, using **neutral syllables** (primarily *bah*), that incorporate repetition, sequence, and silence (rests). Students may or may not, as they wish, perform the chants. Encouraging students to listen and to audiate a specific meter before they perform, however, is essential. An example of a suitable chant in usual triple meter that you may perform for this purpose is notated below.

2. Maintaining a consistent tempo, all students move in a comfortable flowing manner to macrobeats. Discourage toe-tapping and encourage, if necessary, bouncing on heels. Next, all students move to microbeats. Then one group of students moves to macrobeats and another moves to microbeats. Reverse the groups. Do not use music as background to movement. Be alert

that the tempo does not rush or slow. If it does, suggest that students use more space as they move their arms and legs, and that they move their hips from side-to-side rather than moving only their legs and feet.

3. Students *imitate* the teacher by chanting rhythm patterns with **four** underlying macrobeats using **neutral syllables** (primarily *bah*) as they are moving in a comfortable flowing manner to macrobeats and microbeats. Next, students *imitate* the teacher by chanting the rhythm patterns using **rhythm syllables** (*du* and *du-da-di*) as they continue to move to macrobeats and microbeats. Examples of rhythm patterns in usual triple meter are presented below.

4. Individual students, using **neutral syllables**, take turns *improvising* rhythm patterns as the class continues to move and chant macrobeats and microbeats. The patterns, including only **macrobeats and microbeats**, should be no longer or shorter than **four** underlying macrobeats. Next, individual students, using **rhythm syllables** (*du* and *du-da-di*), take turns *improvising* the rhythm patterns as the class continues to move and chant macrobeats and microbeats. Examples of what may be expected of students' rhythm pattern improvisations are notated below in usual triple meter.

5. Individual students, using **neutral syllables**, take turns *improvising* rhythm patterns as the class continues to move and chant macrobeats and microbeats. The patterns, now expanded to include **macrobeats, microbeats, divisions, elongations, and/or rests** should be no longer or shorter than **four** underlying macrobeats. Next, individual students, using **rhythm syllables** (*du* and *du-da-di* and *ta*), take turns *improvising* the rhythm patterns as the class continues to move and chant macrobeats and microbeats. Examples of what may be expected of students' rhythm pattern improvisations are notated below in usual triple meter.

6. Individual students, using **neutral syllables**, take turns *improvising* rhythm patterns as the class continues to move and chant macrobeats and microbeats. The patterns, including **macrobeats, microbeats, divisions, elongations, and/or rests** are now no longer or shorter than **eight** underlying macrobeats. Next, individual students, using **rhythm syllables** (*du* and *du-da-di* and *ta*), take turns *improvising* the rhythm patterns as the class continues to move and chant macrobeats and microbeats. Examples of what may be expected of students' rhythm pattern improvisations are notated below in usual triple meter.

Section C - Usual Combined Meter

1. Perform one or more chants in usual triple meter, using **neutral syllables** (primarily *bah*), that incorporate repetition, sequence, and silence (rests). Students may or may not, as they wish, perform the chants. Encouraging students to listen and to audiate a specific meter before they perform, however, is essential. An example of a suitable chant in usual combined meter that you may perform for this purpose is notated below.

2. Maintaining a consistent tempo, all students move in a comfortable flowing manner to macrobeats. Discourage toe-tapping and encourage, if necessary, bouncing on heels. Next, all students move to microbeats. Then one group of students moves to macrobeats and another moves to microbeats. Reverse the groups. Do not use music as background to movement. Be alert that the tempo does not rush or slow. If it does, suggest that students use more space as they move their arms and legs, and

that they move their hips from side-to-side rather than moving only their legs and feet.

3. Students *imitate* the teacher by chanting rhythm patterns with **four** underlying macrobeats using **neutral syllables** (primarily *bah*) as they are moving in a comfortable flowing manner to macrobeats and microbeats. Next, students *imitate* the teacher by chanting the rhythm patterns using **rhythm syllables** (*du* and *du-de* and *du-da-di*) as they continue to move to macrobeats and microbeats. Examples of rhythm patterns in usual combined meter are presented below.

4. Individual students, using **neutral syllables**, take turns *improvising* rhythm patterns as the class continues to move and chant macrobeats and microbeats. The patterns, including only **macrobeats and microbeats**, should be no longer or shorter than **four** underlying macrobeats. Next, individual students, using **rhythm syllables** (*du* and *du-de* and *du-da-di*), take turns **improvising** the rhythm patterns as the class continues to move and chant macrobeats and microbeats. Examples of what may be expected of students' rhythm pattern improvisations are notated below in usual combined meter.

5. Individual students, using **neutral syllables**, take turns *improvising* rhythm patterns as the class continues to move and chant macrobeats and microbeats. The patterns, now expanded to include **macrobeats, microbeats, divisions, elongations, and/or rests** should be no longer or shorter than **four** underlying macrobeats. Next, individual students, using **rhythm syllables** (*du* and *du*-de and du-*da-di* and *ta*), take turns *improvising* the rhythm patterns as the class continues to move and chant macrobeats and microbeats. Examples of what may be expected of students' rhythm pattern improvisations are notated below in usual combined meter.

6. Individual students, using **neutral syllables**, take turns *improvising* rhythm patterns as the class continues to move and chant macrobeats and microbeats. The patterns, including **macrobeats, microbeats, divisions, elongations, and/or rests** are now no longer or shorter than **eight** underlying macrobeats. Next, individual students, using **rhythm syllables** (*du* and *du-de* and *du-da-di* and *ta*), take turns *improvising* the rhythm patterns as the class continues to move and chant macrobeats and microbeats. Examples of what may be expected of students' rhythm pattern improvisations are notated below in usual combined meter.

Part Four
Tonalities

As with meter in part three, only the fundamental tonalities in western music will be considered. They are major and harmonic minor.

Tonal syllables are the most efficient way for teachers to explain to students how to understand tonalities. Over the centuries, several tonal systems have been advanced. One is best suited, however, for developing audiation, improvisation, and music reading skills. It is traditionally referred to as the "'do' major with a 'la' based minor" system; "do" is the resting tone (tonic) in major, "la" is the resting tone in harmonic minor, "re" is the resting tone in Dorian, and so on.

Tonal Patterns and Tonal Syllables

The three essential tonal patterns in major and harmonic minor are tonic, dominant, and subdominant. **Except for *so* to and from *fa* in the dominant-seventh pattern, stepwise movement is not used.** In major tonality, the syllables in the tonic pattern are "do mi so;" in the dominant-seventh pattern, "so ti re fa;" and in the subdominant pattern, "fa la do." In harmonic minor tonality, the syllables in the tonic pattern are "la do mi;" in the dominant-seventh pattern, "mi si ti re;" and in the subdominant pattern, "la re fa." A tonal pattern includes at least two, usually three, and no more than four tones. The order and sequence of the tones in a pattern is inconsequential. Below are examples of the three patterns in each tonality. Notice that only the tonic patterns are in root position.

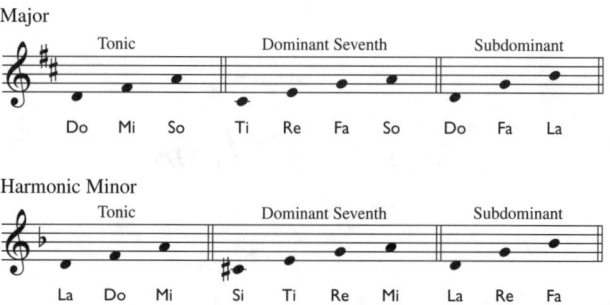

Arpeggiated patterns, not stepwise (scale-wise) patterns, provide students with the most appropriate readiness to improvise harmonically. As will be explained in part eight of this book, after the three essential patterns in the two tonalities are used in harmonic improvisation, then stepwise patterns along with other functions - for example, supertonic, mediant, submediant, subtonic, and leading tone patterns - may be introduced.

Though it is by no means necessary for a teacher or students to memorize or perform scales with syllables, it may be helpful for the teacher to be acquainted conceptually with the chromatic syllables in stepwise scale-form. Ascending they are "do di re ri mi fa fi so si la li ti do." Descending enharmonic syllables are "do ti te la le so se fa mi me re ra do."

Tonal Improvisation

In rhythm, students are auditing and/or moving to macrobeats and microbeats as they imitate and improvise rhythm patterns. In that way, the context of meter that is established by the teacher chanting, and is maintained by students moving, provides structure for rhythm patterns that represent content. Likewise, the context of tonality must be established to provide structure for imitating and improvising tonal patterns that represent content. Also, it is recommended that students move their bodies in a relaxed and flowing manner as they imitate and

PART FOUR: TONALITIES   35

improvise tonally as well as rhythmically. As a result, intonation is bound to improve.

Section A – Major Tonality

The recommended sequential way to expose students to tonal improvisation is described below by step for major tonality. These steps should be completed and reviewed over many class periods. For example, the first step may be introduced during one class period, the second step during the next class period, and so on. Review takes place as needed. Thus, at the beginning of each session tonality context must be re-established.

1. Perform one or more short songs in major tonality that incorporate repetition, sequence, and silence. It is better not to use words with songs, and that is best accomplished by the teacher improvising songs. Students may or may not, as they wish, sing the songs. Encouraging students to listen and to audiate the specific tonality before they perform tonal patterns, however, is important. Examples of appropriate songs in major tonality in the three usual meters are notated below. Songs, of course, need not be sung in every meter to establish the context of major tonality.

   Usual Duple

2. Students *imitate* the teacher by singing tonal patterns using **neutral syllables** (primarily *bum*). Sing a major tonic pattern and ask the whole class or individual students to imitate the pattern. Then sing a major dominant-seventh pattern and ask the whole class or individual students to imitate that pattern. Continue the procedure interspersing tonic and dominant-seventh patterns. Next, students *imitate* the teacher by singing the tonal patterns using **tonal syllables** (*do-mi-so* and *so-ti-re-fa*). Continue the procedure interspersing tonic and dominant-seventh patterns. Examples of major tonic and dominant-seventh patterns are notated on the next page.

Part Four: Tonalities

3. Sing a major tonic pattern and ask the whole class or individual students to *imitate* the pattern using **neutral syllables**. Then sing a major subdominant pattern with individual students or the whole class imitating the pattern. Continue the procedure interspersing tonic and subdominant patterns. Next, students *imitate* the teacher by singing the tonal patterns using **tonal syllables** (*do-mi-so* and *fa-la-do*). Continue the procedure interspersing tonic and subdominant patterns. Examples of subdominant patterns are notated below.

4. The whole class and individual students *imitate* the teacher by singing major tonic, dominant-seventh, and subdominant patterns using **tonal syllables**. Intersperse tonic and dominant-seventh patterns often to sustain the context of major tonality.

5. Sing a major tonic pattern and ask the whole class or individual students in response to *improvise* a different major tonic pattern using **neutral syllables**. Then sing major dominant-seventh and subdominant patterns and ask the whole class or individual students in response to *improvise* different dominant-seventh and subdominant patterns. Remember to intersperse major tonic and dominant-seventh patterns to sustain major tonality.

6. Sing a major tonic pattern and ask the whole class or individual students in response to *improvise* a different major tonic pattern using **tonal syllables**. Then sing major dominant-seventh and subdominant patterns and ask the whole class or individual students in response to *improvise* different dominant-seventh and subdominant patterns. Continue to intersperse major tonic patterns to sustain the context of major tonality.

7. Individual students take turns *improvising* a series of two or three tonic, dominant-seventh, and/or subdominant patterns using **tonal syllables** in response to the teacher or to other students. Each pattern should include at least two tones, usually three tones, and no more than four tones. Tonic patterns should be emphasized.

8. Individual students take turns *improvising* a series of two or three tonic, dominant-seventh, and/or subdominant patterns using **neutral syllables** in response to the teacher or to other students. Each pattern should include at least two tones, usually three tones, and no more than four tones. Tonic patterns should be emphasized.

Section B – Harmonic Minor Tonality

The recommended sequential way to expose students to tonal improvisation is described below by step for harmonic minor tonality. These steps should be completed and reviewed over many class periods. For example, the first step may be introduced during one class period, the second step during the next class period, and so on. Review takes place as needed. Thus, at the beginning of each session tonality context must be re-established.

1. Perform one or more short songs in harmonic minor tonality that incorporate repetition, sequence, and silence. It is better not to use words with songs, and that is best accomplished by

the teacher improvising songs. Students may or may not, as they wish, sing the songs. Encouraging students to listen and to audiate the specific tonality before they perform tonal patterns, however, is important. Examples of appropriate songs in harmonic minor tonality in the three usual meters are notated below. Songs, of course, need not be sung in every meter to establish the context of harmonic minor tonality.

2. Students *imitate* the teacher by singing tonal patterns using **neutral syllables** (primarily *bum*). Sing a harmonic minor tonic pattern and ask the whole class or individual students to imitate the pattern. Then sing a major dominant-seventh pattern and ask the whole class or individual students to imitate that pattern. Continue the procedure interspersing tonic and dominant-seventh patterns. Next, students *imitate* the teacher by singing the tonal patterns using **tonal syllables** (*la-do-mi* and *mi-si-ti-re*). Continue the procedure interspersing tonic and dominant-seventh patterns. Examples of harmonic minor tonic and dominant-seventh patterns are notated below.

3. Sing a harmonic minor tonic pattern and ask the whole class or individual students to *imitate* the pattern using **neutral syllables**. Then sing a harmonic minor subdominant pattern with individual students or the whole class imitating the pattern. Continue the procedure interspersing tonic and subdominant patterns. Next, students *imitate* the teacher by singing the tonal patterns using **tonal syllables** (*la-do-mi* and *re-fa-la*). Continue the procedure interspersing tonic and subdominant patterns. Examples of subdominant patterns are notated on the following page.

Subdominant

Re Fa La Re La Fa Fa Re Re Fa Fa La Re La Fa Re Fa Re La La Re

4. The whole class and individual students *imitate* the teacher by singing harmonic minor tonic, dominant-seventh, and subdominant patterns using **tonal syllables**. Intersperse tonic and dominant-seventh patterns often to sustain the context of harmonic minor tonality.

5. Sing a harmonic minor tonic pattern and ask the whole class or individual students in response to *improvise* a different harmonic minor tonic pattern using **neutral syllables**. Then sing harmonic minor dominant-seventh and subdominant patterns and ask the whole class or individual students in response to *improvise* different dominant-seventh and subdominant patterns. Remember to intersperse harmonic minor tonic and dominant-seventh patterns to sustain harmonic minor tonality.

6. Sing a harmonic minor tonic pattern and ask the whole class or individual students in response to *improvise* a different harmonic minor tonic pattern using **tonal syllables**. Then sing harmonic minor dominant and subdominant patterns and ask the whole class or individual students in response to *improvise* different dominant-seventh and subdominant patterns. Continue to intersperse harmonic minor tonic patterns to sustain the context of harmonic minor tonality.

7. Individual students take turns *improvising* a series of two or three tonic, dominant-seventh, and/or subdominant patterns using **tonal syllables** in response to the teacher or to other students. Each pattern should include at least two tones, usually three tones, and no more than four tones. Tonic patterns should be emphasized.

8. Individual students take turns *improvising* a series of two or three tonic, dominant-seventh, and/or subdominant patterns using **neutral syllables** in response to the teacher or to other students. Each pattern should include at least two tones, usually three tones, and no more than four tones. Tonic patterns should be emphasized.

Part Five
Melodic Patterns

A melodic pattern is a combination of a tonal pattern and a rhythm pattern. It is important that melodic patterns be performed using neutral syllables, because when either tonal or rhythm syllables are used with melodic patterns, students find it difficult to audiate and identify the same tonal pattern performed in different rhythms using different rhythm syllables as indeed being the same tonal pattern. The reverse is also true when using different tonal syllables with the same rhythm pattern. Although melodic patterns are performed using neutral syllables, it is important that students be guided in developing the ability to unconsciously audiate appropriate tonal syllables and rhythm syllables to facilitate their performances as they are performing with neutral syllables.

Melodic Improvisation

Section A – Major Tonality and Usual Duple Meter

The recommended sequential way to expose students to improvising melodic patterns is described below by step for major tonality and usual duple meter. Because all steps will not be completed during one class period, at the beginning of each session both tonality context and meter context must be re-established.

1. Perform one or more songs in major tonality and usual duple meter so that students may audiate the appropriate tonality and meter contexts before they perform melodic patterns. Shorter

but equally effective songs as those presented in part four in major and usual duple meter for establishing tonality and meter contexts are notated below. Songs, of course, may be transposed to match singing ranges and tessituras.

2. Students *imitate* the teacher by singing melodic patterns using **neutral syllables**. The patterns, no longer or shorter than **four** underlying macrobeats, should include only **major tonic or dominant-seventh** pattern pitches for each underlying macrobeat and only **usual duple meter macrobeats and/or microbeats**. Examples of melodic patterns in major tonality and usual duple meter are notated below.

3. Students respond to the teacher or to one another by *improvising* melodic patterns using **neutral syllables**. The patterns, no longer or shorter than **four** underlying macrobeats, should include only **major tonic or dominant-seventh** pattern pitches for each underlying macrobeat and only **usual duple meter macrobeats and/or microbeats**.

4. Students *imitate* the teacher by singing longer melodic patterns using **neutral syllables**. The patterns, based on **six or eight** underlying macrobeats, should include only **major tonic, dominant-seventh, or subdominant** pattern pitches for each

PART FIVE: MELODIC PATTERNS 45

underlying macrobeat and only **usual duple meter macrobeats, microbeats, and/or divisions**. Examples of melodic patterns in major tonality and usual duple meter are notated below.

5. Students respond to the teacher or to one another by *improvising* longer melodic patterns using **neutral syllables**. The patterns, based on **six or eight** underlying macrobeats, should include only **major tonic, dominant-seventh, or subdominant** pattern pitches for each underlying macrobeat and only **usual duple meter macrobeats, microbeats, and/or divisions**.

6. Students *imitate* the teacher by singing melodic patterns based on **six or eight** underlying macrobeats using **neutral syllables**. Each series should only **include major tonic, dominant-seventh, or subdominant** pattern pitches for each underlying macrobeat and only **usual duple meter macrobeats, microbeats, divisions, elongations, and/or rests**. Examples of melodic patterns in major tonality and usual duple meter are notated below.

7. Students respond to the teacher or to one another by *improvising* melodic patterns based on **six or eight** underlying macrobeats using **neutral syllables**. Each series should include only **major tonic, dominant-seventh, or subdominant** pattern pitches for each underlying macrobeat and only **usual duple meter macrobeats, microbeats, divisions, elongations, and/or rests**.

8. Students *imitate* the teacher by singing melodic patterns based on **six or eight** underlying macrobeats using **neutral syllables**. Each series should include primarily **major tonic, dominant-seventh, or subdominant** pattern pitches for each underlying macrobeat and **usual duple meter macrobeats, microbeats, divisions, elongations, upbeats, and/or rests. Non-harmonic tones**, particularly those **moving by step**, now should be included. Examples of melodic patterns in major tonality and usual duple meter are notated below.

9. Students respond to the teacher or to one another by *improvising* melodic patterns based on **six or eight** underlying macrobeats using **neutral syllables**. Each series should include primarily **major tonic, dominant-seventh, or subdominant** pattern pitches for each underlying macrobeat and **usual duple meter macrobeats, microbeats, divisions, elongations, upbeats, and/or rests. Non-harmonic tones**, particularly those **moving by step**, should be included.

Section B – Major Tonality and Usual Triple Meter

The recommended sequential way to expose students to improvising melodic patterns is described below by step for major tonality and usual triple meter. Because all steps will not be completed during one class period, at the beginning of each session both tonality context and meter context must be re-established.

1. Perform one or more songs in major tonality and usual triple meter so that students may audiate the appropriate tonality and meter contexts before they perform melodic patterns. Shorter

but equally effective songs as those presented in part four in major and usual triple meter for establishing tonality and meter contexts are notated below. Songs, of course, may be transposed to match singing ranges and tessituras.

2. Students *imitate* the teacher by singing melodic patterns using **neutral syllables**. The patterns, no longer or shorter than **four** underlying macrobeats, should include only **major tonic or dominant-seventh** pattern pitches for each underlying macrobeat and only **usual triple meter macrobeats and/or microbeats**. Examples of melodic patterns in major tonality and usual triple meter are notated below.

3. Students respond to the teacher or to one another by *improvising* melodic patterns using **neutral syllables**. The patterns, no longer or shorter than **four** underlying macrobeats, should include only **major tonic or dominant-seventh** pattern pitches for each underlying macrobeat and only **usual triple meter macrobeats and/or microbeats**.

4. Students *imitate* the teacher by singing longer melodic patterns using **neutral syllables**. The patterns, based on **six or eight** underlying macrobeats, should include only **major tonic, dominant-seventh, or subdominant** pattern pitches for each

underlying macrobeat and only **usual triple meter macrobeats, microbeats, and/or divisions.** Examples of melodic patterns in major tonality and usual triple meter are notated below.

5. Students respond to the teacher or to one another by *improvising* longer melodic patterns using **neutral syllables.** The patterns, based on **six or eight** underlying macrobeats, should include only **major tonic, dominant-seventh, or subdominant** pattern pitches for each underlying macrobeat and only **usual triple meter macrobeats, microbeats, and/or divisions.**

6. Students *imitate* the teacher by singing melodic patterns based on **six or eight** underlying macrobeats using **neutral syllables.** Each series should only **include major tonic, dominant-seventh, or subdominant** pattern pitches for each underlying macrobeat and only **usual triple meter macrobeats, microbeats, divisions, elongations, and/or rests.** Examples of melodic patterns in major tonality and usual triple meter are notated below.

7. Students respond to the teacher or to one another by *improvising* melodic patterns based on **six or eight** underlying macrobeats using **neutral syllables.** Each series should only **include major tonic, dominant-seventh, or subdominant** pattern pitches for each underlying macrobeat and only **usual triple meter macrobeats, microbeats, divisions, elongations, and/or rests.**

PART FIVE: MELODIC PATTERNS

8. Students *imitate* the teacher by singing melodic patterns based on **six or eight** underlying macrobeats using **neutral syllables**. Each series should include primarily **major tonic, dominant-seventh, or subdominant** pattern pitches for each underlying macrobeat and **usual triple meter macrobeats, microbeats, divisions, elongations, upbeats, and/or rests**. **Non-harmonic tones**, particularly those **moving by step**, now should be included. Examples of melodic patterns in major tonality and usual triple meter are notated below.

9. Students respond to the teacher or to one another by *improvising* melodic patterns based on **six or eight** underlying macrobeats using **neutral syllables**. Each series should include primarily **major tonic, dominant-seventh, or subdominant** pattern pitches for each underlying macrobeat and **usual triple meter macrobeats, microbeats, divisions, elongations, upbeats, and/or rests**. **Non-harmonic tones**, particularly those **moving by step**, should be included.

Section C – Major Tonality and Usual Combined Meter

The recommended sequential way to expose students to improvising melodic patterns is described below by step for major tonality and usual combined meter. Because all steps will not be completed during one class period, at the beginning of each session both tonality context and meter context must be re-established.

1. Perform one or more songs in major tonality and usual combined meter so that students may audiate the appropriate tonality and meter contexts before they perform melodic

patterns. Shorter but equally effective songs as those presented in part four in major and usual combined meter for establishing tonality and meter contexts are notated below. Songs, of course, may be transposed to match singing ranges and tessituras.

2. Students *imitate* the teacher by singing melodic patterns using **neutral syllables**. The patterns, no longer or shorter than **four** underlying macrobeats, should include only **major tonic or dominant-seventh** pattern pitches for each underlying macrobeat and only **usual combined meter macrobeats and/or microbeats**. Examples of melodic patterns in major tonality and usual combined meter are notated below.

3. Students respond to the teacher or to one another by *improvising* melodic patterns using **neutral syllables**. The patterns, no longer or shorter than **four** underlying macrobeats, should include only **major tonic or dominant-seventh** pattern pitches for each underlying macrobeat and only **usual combined meter macrobeats and/or microbeats**.

4. Students *imitate* the teacher by singing longer melodic patterns using **neutral syllables**. The patterns, based on **six or eight** underlying macrobeats, should include only **major tonic, dominant-seventh, or subdominant** pattern pitches for each underlying macrobeat and only **usual combined meter**

macrobeats, microbeats, and/or divisions. Examples of melodic patterns in major tonality and usual combined meter are notated below.

5. Students respond to the teacher or to one another by *improvising* longer melodic patterns using **neutral syllables**. The patterns, based on **six or eight** underlying macrobeats, should include only **major tonic, dominant-seventh, or subdominant** pattern pitches for each underlying macrobeat and only **usual combined meter macrobeats, microbeats, and/or divisions.**

6. Students *imitate* the teacher by singing melodic patterns based on **six or eight** underlying macrobeats using **neutral syllables**. Each series should only **include major tonic, dominant-seventh, or subdominant** pattern pitches for each underlying macrobeat and only **usual combined meter macrobeats, microbeats, divisions, elongations, and/or rests.** Examples of melodic patterns in major tonality and usual combined meter are notated below.

7. Students respond to the teacher or to one another by *improvising* melodic patterns based on **six or eight** underlying macrobeats using **neutral syllables**. Each series should include only **major tonic, dominant-seventh, or subdominant** pattern pitches for each underlying macrobeat and only **usual**

combined meter macrobeats, microbeats, divisions, elongations, and/or rests.

8. Students *imitate* the teacher by singing melodic patterns based on **six or eight** underlying macrobeats using **neutral syllables**. Each series should include primarily **major tonic, dominant-seventh, or subdominant** pattern pitches for each underlying macrobeat and **usual combined meter macrobeats, microbeats, divisions, elongations, upbeats, and/or rests**. **Non-harmonic tones**, particularly those **moving by step**, now should be included. Examples of melodic patterns in major tonality and usual combined meter are notated below.

9. Students respond to the teacher or to one another by *improvising* melodic patterns based on **six or eight** underlying macrobeats using **neutral syllables**. Each series should include primarily **major tonic, dominant-seventh, or subdominant** pattern pitches for each underlying macrobeat and **usual combined meter macrobeats, microbeats, divisions, elongations, upbeats, and/or rests**. **Non-harmonic tones**, particularly those **moving by step**, should be included.

Section D – Harmonic Minor Tonality and Usual Duple Meter

The recommended sequential way to expose students to improvising melodic patterns is described below by step for harmonic minor tonality and usual duple meter. Because all steps will not be completed during one class period, at the beginning of each session both tonality context and meter context must be re-established.

PART FIVE: MELODIC PATTERNS   53

1. Perform one or more songs in harmonic minor tonality and usual duple meter so that students may audiate the appropriate tonality and meter contexts before they perform melodic patterns. Shorter but equally effective songs as those presented in part four in harmonic minor and usual duple meter for establishing tonality and meter contexts are notated below. Songs, of course, may be transposed to match singing ranges and tessituras.

2. Students *imitate* the teacher by singing melodic patterns using **neutral syllables**. The patterns, no longer or shorter than **four** underlying macrobeats, should include only **harmonic minor tonic or dominant-seventh** pattern pitches for each underlying macrobeat and only **usual duple meter macrobeats and/or microbeats**. Examples of melodic patterns in harmonic minor tonality and usual duple meter are notated below.

3. Students respond to the teacher or to one another by *improvising* melodic patterns using **neutral syllables**. The patterns, no longer or shorter than **four** underlying macrobeats, should include only **harmonic minor tonic or dominant-seventh** pattern pitches for each underlying macrobeat and only **usual**

duple meter macrobeats and/or microbeats.

4. Students *imitate* the teacher by singing longer melodic patterns using **neutral syllables**. The patterns, based on **six or eight** underlying macrobeats, should include only **harmonic minor tonic, dominant-seventh, or subdominant** pattern pitches for each underlying macrobeat and only **usual duple meter macrobeats, microbeats, and/or divisions**. Examples of melodic patterns in harmonic minor tonality and usual duple meter are notated below.

5. Students respond to the teacher or to one another by *improvising* longer melodic patterns using **neutral syllables**. The patterns, based on **six or eight** underlying macrobeats, should include only **harmonic minor tonic, dominant-seventh, or subdominant** pattern pitches for each underlying macrobeat and only **usual duple meter macrobeats, microbeats, and/or divisions**.

6. Students *imitate* the teacher by singing melodic patterns based on **six or eight** underlying macrobeats using **neutral syllables**. Each series should include only **harmonic minor tonic, dominant-seventh, or subdominant** pattern pitches for each underlying macrobeat and only **usual duple meter macrobeats, microbeats, divisions, elongations, and/or rests**. Examples of melodic patterns in harmonic minor tonality and usual duple meter are notated below.

PART FIVE: MELODIC PATTERNS   55

7. Students respond to the teacher or to one another by *improvising* melodic patterns based on **six or eight** underlying macrobeats using **neutral syllables**. Each series should include only **harmonic minor tonic, dominant-seventh, or subdominant** pattern pitches for each underlying macrobeat and only **usual duple meter macrobeats, microbeats, divisions, elongations, and/or rests.**

8. Students *imitate* the teacher by singing melodic patterns based on **six or eight** underlying macrobeats using **neutral syllables**. Each series should include primarily **harmonic minor tonic, dominant-seventh, or subdominant** pattern pitches for each underlying macrobeat and **usual duple meter macrobeats, microbeats, divisions, elongations, upbeats, and/or rests.** Non-harmonic tones, particularly those **moving by step**, now should be included. Examples of melodic patterns in harmonic minor tonality and usual duple meter are notated below.

9. Students respond to the teacher or to one another by *improvising* melodic patterns based on **six or eight** underlying macrobeats using **neutral syllables**. Each series should include primarily **harmonic minor tonic, dominant-seventh, or subdominant** pattern pitches for each underlying macrobeat and **usual duple meter macrobeats, microbeats, divisions, elongations, upbeats, and/or rests.** Non-harmonic tones, particularly those **moving by step**, should be included.

Section E – Harmonic Minor Tonality and Usual Triple Meter

The recommended sequential way to expose students to improvising melodic patterns is described below by step for harmonic minor tonality and usual triple meter. Because all steps will not be completed during one class period, at the beginning of each session both tonality context and meter context must be re-established.

1. Perform one or more songs in harmonic minor tonality and usual triple meter so that students may audiate the appropriate tonality and meter contexts before they perform melodic patterns. Shorter but equally effective songs as those presented in part four in harmonic minor and usual triple meter for establishing tonality and meter contexts are notated below. Songs, of course, may be transposed to match singing ranges and tessituras.

2. Students *imitate* the teacher by singing melodic patterns using **neutral syllables**. The patterns, no longer or shorter than **four** underlying macrobeats, should include only **harmonic minor tonic or dominant-seventh** pattern pitches for each underlying macrobeat and only **usual triple meter macrobeats and/or microbeats**. Examples of melodic patterns in harmonic minor tonality and usual triple meter are notated below.

PART FIVE: MELODIC PATTERNS

3. Students respond to the teacher or to one another by *improvising* melodic patterns using **neutral syllables**. The patterns, no longer or shorter than **four** underlying macrobeats, should include only **harmonic minor tonic or dominant-seventh** pattern pitches for each underlying macrobeat and only **usual triple meter macrobeats and/or microbeats**.

4. Students *imitate* the teacher by singing longer melodic patterns using **neutral syllables**. The patterns, based on **six or eight** underlying macrobeats, should include only **harmonic minor tonic, dominant-seventh, or subdominant** pattern pitches for each underlying macrobeat and only **usual triple meter macrobeats, microbeats, and/or divisions**. Examples of melodic patterns in harmonic minor tonality and usual triple meter are notated below.

5. Students respond to the teacher or to one another by *improvising* longer melodic patterns using **neutral syllables**. The patterns, based on **six or eight** underlying macrobeats, should include only **harmonic minor tonic, dominant-seventh, or subdominant** pattern pitches for each underlying macrobeat and only **usual triple meter macrobeats, microbeats, and/or divisions**.

6. Students *imitate* the teacher by singing melodic patterns based on **six or eight** underlying macrobeats using **neutral syllables**. Each series should include only **harmonic minor tonic, dominant-seventh, or subdominant** pattern pitches for each underlying macrobeat and only **usual triple meter macrobeats, microbeats, divisions, elongations, and/or rests**. Examples of melodic patterns in harmonic minor tonality and usual triple meter are notated on the following page.

7. Students respond to the teacher or to one another by *improvising* melodic patterns based on **six or eight** underlying macrobeats using **neutral syllables**. Each series should include only **harmonic minor tonic, dominant-seventh, or subdominant** pattern pitches for each underlying macrobeat and only **usual triple meter macrobeats, microbeats, divisions, elongations, and/or rests.**

8. Students *imitate* the teacher by singing melodic patterns based on **six or eight** underlying macrobeats using **neutral syllables**. Each series should include primarily **harmonic minor tonic, dominant-seventh, or subdominant** pattern pitches for each underlying macrobeat and **usual triple meter macrobeats, microbeats, divisions, elongations, upbeats, and/or rests. Non-harmonic tones**, particularly those **moving by step**, now should be included. Examples of melodic patterns in harmonic minor tonality and usual triple meter are notated below.

9. Students respond to the teacher or to one another by *improvising* melodic patterns based on **six or eight** underlying macrobeats using **neutral syllables**. Each series should include primarily **harmonic minor tonic, dominant-seventh, or subdominant** pattern pitches for each underlying macrobeat and **usual triple meter macrobeats, microbeats, divisions,**

elongations, upbeats, and/or rests. Non-harmonic tones, particularly those moving by step, should be included.

Section F – Harmonic Minor Tonality and Usual Combined Meter

The recommended sequential way to expose students to improvising melodic patterns is described below by step for harmonic minor tonality and usual combined meter. Because all steps will not be completed during one class period, at the beginning of each session both tonality context and meter context must be re-established.

1. Perform one or more songs in harmonic minor tonality and usual combined meter so that students may audiate the appropriate tonality and meter contexts before they perform melodic patterns. Shorter but equally effective songs as those presented in part four in harmonic minor and usual combined meter for establishing tonality and meter contexts are notated below. Songs, of course, may be transposed to match singing ranges and tessituras.

2. Students *imitate* the teacher by singing melodic patterns using **neutral syllables**. The patterns, no longer or shorter than **four** underlying macrobeats, should include only **harmonic minor tonic or dominant-seventh** pattern pitches for each underlying macrobeat and only **usual combined meter macrobeats and/or microbeats**. Examples of melodic patterns in harmonic minor tonality and usual combined meter are notated on the next page.

3. Students respond to the teacher or to one another by *improvising* melodic patterns using **neutral syllables**. The patterns, no longer or shorter than **four** underlying macrobeats, should include only **harmonic minor tonic or dominant-seventh** pattern pitches for each underlying macrobeat and only **usual combined meter macrobeats and/or microbeats**.

4. Students *imitate* the teacher by singing longer melodic patterns using **neutral syllables**. The patterns, based on **six or eight** underlying macrobeats, should include only **harmonic minor tonic, dominant-seventh, or subdominant** pattern pitches for each underlying macrobeat and only **usual combined meter macrobeats, microbeats, and/or divisions**. Examples of melodic patterns in harmonic minor tonality and usual combined meter are notated below.

5. Students respond to the teacher or to one another by *improvising* longer melodic patterns using **neutral syllables**. The patterns, based on **six or eight** underlying macrobeats, should include only **harmonic minor tonic, dominant-seventh, or subdominant** pattern pitches for each underlying macrobeat and only **usual combined meter macrobeats, microbeats, and/or divisions**.

PART FIVE: MELODIC PATTERNS

6. Students *imitate* the teacher by singing melodic patterns based on **six or eight** underlying macrobeats using **neutral syllables**. Each series should include only **harmonic minor tonic, dominant-seventh, or subdominant** pattern pitches for each underlying macrobeat and only **usual combined meter macrobeats, microbeats, divisions, elongations, and/or rests**. Examples of melodic patterns in harmonic minor tonality and usual combined meter are notated below.

7. Students respond to the teacher or to one another by *improvising* melodic patterns based on **six or eight** underlying macrobeats using **neutral syllables**. Each series should include only **harmonic minor tonic, dominant-seventh, or subdominant** pattern pitches for each underlying macrobeat and only **usual combined meter macrobeats, microbeats, divisions, elongations, and/or rests**.

8. Students *imitate* the teacher by singing melodic patterns based on **six or eight** underlying macrobeats using **neutral syllables**. Each series should include primarily **harmonic minor tonic, dominant-seventh, or subdominant** pattern pitches for each underlying macrobeat and **usual combined meter macrobeats, microbeats, divisions, elongations, upbeats, and/or rests**. **Non-harmonic tones**, particularly those **moving by step**, now should be included. Examples of melodic patterns in harmonic minor tonality and usual combined meter are notated below.

9. Students respond to the teacher or to one another by *improvising* melodic patterns based on **six or eight** underlying macrobeats using **neutral syllables**. Each series should include primarily **harmonic minor tonic, dominant-seventh, or subdominant** pattern pitches for each underlying macrobeat and **usual combined meter macrobeats, microbeats, divisions, elongations, upbeats, and/or rests**. Non-harmonic tones, particularly those **moving by step**, should be included.

Part Six
Harmonic Patterns

Harmonic Patterns

The harmonic patterns in major and harmonic minor tonalities that were used in the research for the development of the *Harmonic Improvisation Readiness Record* and the *Rhythm Improvisation Readiness Record* are notated below. They represent the fundamental harmonic patterns in the two tonalities. Each harmonic pattern is separated by double vertical lines.

HARMONIC MINOR

All of the harmonic patterns consist of three chords (triads), with three pitches in each chord but without intended rhythm, and each harmonic pattern begins and ends with the tonic chord. No melody is supplied with the harmonic patterns, although the upper voice could be interpreted as a melody.

As will be clarified in part seven, after students learn by rote to audiate each middle chord in every harmonic pattern as it relates to the established tonic chord in a tonality, it is relatively easy for them to begin audiating two or more middle chords contiguously in relation to an established tonic chord. Then, with sufficient experience audiating those familiar harmonic patterns, students will make inferences and improvise longer melodic patterns in various tonalities, meters, and styles.

Part Seven
Harmonic Improvisation - A

To improvise a melody over one or more harmonic patterns, it is best that students initially acquire a vocabulary of tonal patterns in major and harmonic minor tonalities and a vocabulary of rhythm patterns in usual duple, usual triple, and usual combined meters. This means that students need to be able to perform tonal patterns using movable "do" tonal syllables with a "la" based minor, and rhythm patterns using rhythm syllables based on beat functions. It is also beneficial if students are familiar with the proper names and syllable names of the patterns so they can verbally identify as well as audiate tonic, dominant-seventh, and subdominant patterns in major and harmonic minor tonalities, and macrobeats, microbeats, divisions, elongations, rests, and upbeats in usual duple, usual triple, and usual combined meters. All of this has already been accomplished in parts three and four.

Just as tonal patterns must be learned within the context of a tonality and rhythm patterns in the context of a meter, so harmonic patterns must be learned within the context of a tonality and a meter. Thus, the tonality and keyality and the meter and tempo in which the harmonic patterns are to be audiated should be established before teaching students to improvise melodies over harmonic progressions. Although all examples in this part of the book are in usual duple meter, they may serve as models for improvising in other meters.

Section A – Major: Tonic/Dominant-Seventh/Tonic

Student participation begins as outlined by step in the following sequential manner:

1. The class is divided into three groups of students. **Using tonal syllables first and then neutral syllables**, in major tonality, Group 1 sings the root of the tonic chord, Group 2 sings the third of the tonic chord, and Group 3 sings the fifth of the tonic chord. All groups sing simultaneously so that the sound of the tonic chord can be audiated.

2. After a pause, Group 1 moves to the third of the dominant-seventh chord, Group 2 moves to the seventh of the dominant-seventh chord, and Group 3 moves to the root of the dominant-seventh chord. Direct students to audiate the sound of the dominant-seventh chord.

3. After a pause, the groups move back to the tonic chord. All of this is done through audiation and, of course, no notation is used. The chord progression tonic/dominant-seventh/tonic in major tonality is notated below.

4. All students as a group move their bodies to macrobeats. This is repeated until they feel comfortable audiating a span of six macrobeats.

5. Now students as a group sing the roots **using tonal syllables first and then neutral syllables** to the tonic/dominant-seventh/tonic chords over six underlying macrobeats as notated below.

PART SEVEN: HARMONIC IMPROVISATION - A 67

6. After you demonstrate in a comfortable singing range how to improvise melodic patterns, all students singing together using **neutral syllables** improvise their individual melodies to the familiar chord progression. The melodies may incorporate macrobeats, microbeats, divisions, and elongations. For the first two underlying macrobeats, the melody is based on only **major tonic** pattern pitches; for the third and fourth underlying macrobeats, the melody is based on only **major dominant-seventh** pattern pitches; and for the fifth and sixth underlying macrobeats, the melody is based on only **major tonic** pattern pitches. **No non-harmonic tones are used at this time.** When the performance of the ensemble sounds consonant, you know that all students are singing acceptable pitches.

7. As the class sings the chord progression of major tonic/dominant-seventh/tonic over six underlying macrobeats, individual students take turns improvising a solo melody. Examples of individual students' appropriate improvisations are notated below.

8. Before moving on, repeat in abbreviated fashion what has been done, but with the groups changing parts for the chords. For example, Group 1 sings what Group 2 sang, Group 2 sings what Group 3 sang, and Group 3 sings what Group 1 sang.

Section B – Major: Tonic/Subdominant/Tonic

Student participation begins as outlined by step in the following sequential manner:

1. The class is divided into three groups of students. **Using tonal syllables first and then neutral syllables**, in major tonality, Group 1 sings the root of the tonic chord, Group 2 sings the third of the tonic chord, and Group 3 sings the fifth of the tonic chord. All groups sing simultaneously so that the sound of the tonic chord can be audiated.

2. After a pause, Group 1 moves to the fifth of the subdominant chord, Group 2 moves to the root of the subdominant chord, and Group 3 moves to the third of the subdominant chord. Direct students to audiate the sound of the subdominant chord.

3. After a pause, the groups move back to the tonic chord. All of this is done through audiation and, of course, no notation is used. The chord progression tonic/subdominant/ tonic in major tonality is notated below.

4. All students as a group move their bodies to macrobeats. This is repeated until they feel comfortable audiating a span of six macrobeats.

PART SEVEN: HARMONIC IMPROVISATION - A   69

5. Now students as a group sing the roots **using tonal syllables first and then neutral syllables** to the tonic/subdominant/tonic chords over six underlying macrobeats as notated below.

6. After you demonstrate in a comfortable singing range how to improvise melodic patterns, all students singing together using **neutral syllables** improvise their individual melodies to the familiar chord progression. The melodies may incorporate macrobeats, microbeats, divisions, and elongations. For the first two underlying macrobeats, the melody is based on only **major tonic** pattern pitches; for the third and fourth underlying macrobeats, the melody is based on only **major subdominant** pattern pitches; and for the fifth and sixth underlying macrobeats, the melody is based on only **major tonic** pattern pitches. **No non-harmonic tones are used at this time.** When the performance of the ensemble sounds consonant, you know that all students are singing acceptable pitches.

7. As the class sings the chord progression of major tonic/subdominant/tonic over six underlying macrobeats, individual students take turns improvising a solo melody. Examples of individual students' appropriate improvisations are notated below.

8. Before moving on, the groups change parts singing the chords.

Section C - Harmonic Minor: Tonic/Dominant-Seventh/Tonic

Student participation begins as outlined by step in the following sequential manner:

1. The class is divided into three groups of students. **Using tonal syllables first and then neutral syllables**, in harmonic minor tonality, Group 1 sings the root of the tonic chord, Group 2 sings the third of the tonic chord, and Group 3 sings the fifth of the tonic chord. All groups sing simultaneously so that the sound of the tonic chord can be audiated.

2. After a pause, Group 1 moves to the third of the dominant-seventh chord, Group 2 moves to the seventh of the dominant-seventh chord, and Group 3 moves to the root of the dominant-seventh chord. Direct students to audiate the sound of the dominant-seventh chord.

3. After a pause, the groups move back to the tonic chord. All of this is done through audiation and, of course, no notation is used. The chord progression tonic/dominant-seventh/tonic in harmonic minor tonality is notated below.

4. All students as a group move their bodies to macrobeats. This is repeated until they feel comfortable audiating a span of six macrobeats.

PART SEVEN: HARMONIC IMPROVISATION - A

5. Now students as a group sing the roots **using tonal syllables first and then neutral syllables** to the tonic/dominant-seventh/tonic chords over six underlying macrobeats as notated below.

6. After you demonstrate in a comfortable singing range how to improvise melodic patterns, all students singing together using **neutral syllables** improvise their individual melodies to the familiar chord progression. The melodies may incorporate macrobeats, microbeats, divisions, and elongations. For the first two underlying macrobeats, the melody is based on only **harmonic minor tonic** pattern pitches; for the third and fourth underlying macrobeats, the melody is based on only **harmonic minor dominant-seventh** pattern pitches; and for the fifth and sixth underlying macrobeats, the melody is based on only **harmonic minor tonic** pattern pitches. **No non-harmonic tones are used at this time.** When the performance of the ensemble sounds consonant, you know that all students are singing acceptable pitches.

7. As the class sings the chord progression of harmonic minor tonic/dominant-seventh//tonic over six underlying macrobeats, individual students take turns improvising a solo melody. Examples of individual students' appropriate improvisations are notated below.

8. Before moving on, repeat in abbreviated fashion what has been done, but with the groups changing parts for the chords. For example, Group 1 sings what Group 2 sang, Group 2 sings what Group 3 sang, and Group 3 sings what Group 1 sang.

Section D – Harmonic Minor: Tonic/Subdominant/Tonic

Student participation begins as outlined by step in the following sequential manner:

1. The class is divided into three groups of students. **Using tonal syllables first and then neutral syllables**, in harmonic minor tonality, Group 1 sings the root of the tonic chord, Group 2 sings the third of the tonic chord, and Group 3 sings the fifth of the tonic chord. All groups sing simultaneously so that the sound of the tonic chord can be audiated.

2. After a pause, Group 1 moves to the fifth of the subdominant chord, Group 2 moves to the root of the subdominant chord, and Group 3 moves to the third of the subdominant chord. Direct students to audiate the sound of the subdominant chord.

3. After a pause, the groups move back to the tonic chord. All of this is done through audiation and, of course, no notation is used. The chord progression tonic/subdominant/ tonic in harmonic minor tonality is notated below.

PART SEVEN: HARMONIC IMPROVISATION - A   73

4. All students as a group move their bodies to macrobeats. This is repeated until they feel comfortable audiating a span of six macrobeats.

5. Now students as a group sing the roots **using tonal syllables first and then neutral syllables** to the tonic/subdominant/tonic chords over six underlying macrobeats as notated below.

6. After you demonstrate in a comfortable singing range how to improvise melodicpatterns, all students singing together using **neutral syllables** improvise their individual melodies to the familiar chord progression. The melodies may incorporate macrobeats, microbeats, divisions, and elongations. For the first two underlying macrobeats, the melody is based on only **harmonic minor tonic** pattern pitches; for the third and fourth underlying macrobeats, the melody is based on only **harmonic minor subdominant** pattern pitches; and for the fifth and sixth underlying macrobeats, the melody is based on only **harmonic minor tonic** pattern pitches. **No non-harmonic tones are used at this time.** When the performance of the ensemble sounds consonant, you know that all students are singing acceptable pitches.

7. As the class sings the chord progression of harmonic minor tonic/subdominant/tonic over six underlying macrobeats, individual students take turns improvising a solo melody. Examples of individual students' appropriate improvisations are notated below.

8. Before moving on, the groups change parts singing the chords.

Section E – Major: Tonic/Subdominant/Dominant-Seventh/Tonic

Student participation begins as outlined by step in the following sequential manner:

1. The class is divided into three groups of students. **Using tonal syllables first and then neutral syllables,** in major tonality, Group 1 sings the root of the tonic chord, Group 2 sings the third of the tonic chord, and Group 3 sings the fifth of the tonic chord. All groups sing simultaneously so that the sound of the tonic chord can be audiated.

2. After a pause, Group 1 moves to the fifth of the subdominant chord, Group 2 moves to the root of the subdominant chord, and Group 3 moves to the third of the subdominant chord. Direct students to audiate the sound of the subdominant chord.

3. After a pause, Group 1 moves to the third of the dominant-seventh chord, Group 2 moves to the seventh of the dominant-seventh chord, and Group 3 moves to the root of the dominant-seventh chord. Direct students to audiate the sound of the dominant-seventh chord.

PART SEVEN: HARMONIC IMPROVISATION - A   75

4. After a pause, the groups move back to the tonic chord. All of this is done through audiation and, of course, no notation is used. The chord progression tonic/subdominant/seventh/tonic in major tonality is notated below.

5. All students as a group move their bodies to macrobeats. This is repeated until they feel comfortable audiating a span of eight macrobeats.

6. Now students as a group sing the roots **using tonal syllables first and then neutral syllables** to the tonic/subdominant/dominant-seventh/tonic chords over eight underlying macrobeats as notated below.

7. After you demonstrate in a comfortable singing range how to improvise melodic patterns, all students singing together using **neutral syllables** improvise their individual melodies to the familiar chord progression. The melodies may incorporate macrobeats, microbeats, divisions, and elongations. For the first two underlying macrobeats, the melody is based on only **major tonic** pattern pitches; for the third and fourth underlying macrobeats, the melody is based on only **major subdominant** pattern pitches; for the fifth and sixth underlying macrobeats, the melody is based on only **major dominant-seventh** pattern pitches; and for the seventh and eight underlying macrobeats, the melody is based on only **major tonic** pattern pitches. **No non-harmonic tones are used at this time.** When the

performance of the ensemble sounds consonant, you know that all students are singing acceptable pitches.

8. As the class sings the chord progression of major tonic/subdominant/dominant-seventh/tonic over eight underlying macrobeats, individual students take turns improvising a solo melody. Examples of individual students' appropriate improvisations are notated below.

9. Before moving on, the groups change parts singing the chords.

Section F – Major: Tonic/Dominant-Seventh/Subdominant/Tonic

Student participation begins as outlined by step in the following sequential manner:

1. The class is divided into three groups of students. **Using tonal syllables first and then neutral syllables**, in major tonality, Group 1 sings the root of the tonic chord, Group 2 sings the third of the tonic chord, and Group 3 sings the fifth of the tonic chord. All groups sing simultaneously so that the sound of the tonic chord can be audiated.

Part Seven: Harmonic Improvisation - A

2. After a pause, Group 1 moves to the third of the dominant-seventh chord, Group 2 moves to the seventh of the dominant-seventh chord, and Group 3 moves to the root of the dominant-seventh chord. Direct students to audiate the sound of the dominant-seventh chord.

3. After a pause, Group 1 moves to the fifth of the subdominant chord, Group 2 moves to the root of the subdominant chord, and Group 3 moves to the third of the subdominant chord. Direct students to audiate the sound of the subdominant chord.

4. After a pause, the groups move back to the tonic chord. All of this is done through audiation and, of course, no notation is used. The chord progression tonic/dominant-seventh/subdominant/tonic in major tonality is notated below.

5. All students as a group move their bodies to macrobeats. This is repeated until they feel comfortable audiating a span of eight macrobeats.

6. Now students as a group sing the roots **using tonal syllables first and then neutral syllables** to the tonic/subdominant/dominant-seventh/tonic chords over eight underlying macrobeats as notated below.

7. After you demonstrate in a comfortable singing range how to improvise melodic patterns, all students singing together using **neutral syllables** improvise their individual melodies to the familiar chord progression. The melodies may incorporate macrobeats, microbeats, divisions, and elongations. For the first two underlying macrobeats, the melody is based on only **major**

tonic pattern pitches; for the third and fourth underlying macrobeats, the melody is based on only **major dominant-seventh** pattern pitches; for the fifth and sixth underlying macrobeats, the melody is based on only **major subdominant** pattern pitches; and for the seventh and eight underlying macrobeats, the melody is based on only **major tonic** pattern pitches. **No non-harmonic tones are used at this time.** When the performance of the ensemble sounds consonant, you know that all students are singing acceptable pitches.

8. As the class sings the chord progression of major tonic/ dominant-seventh/ subdominant/tonic over eight underlying macrobeats, individual students take turns improvising a solo melody. Examples of individual students' appropriate improvisations are notated below.

9. Before moving on, the groups change parts singing the chords.

PART SEVEN: HARMONIC IMPROVISATION - A   79

Section G - Harmonic Minor: Tonic/Subdominant/ Dominant-Seventh/Tonic

Student participation begins as outlined by step in the following sequential manner:

1. As before, the class is divided into three groups of students. **Using tonal syllables first and then neutral syllables**, in harmonic minor tonality, Group 1 sings the root of the tonic chord, Group 2 sings the third of the tonic chord, and Group 3 sings the fifth of the tonic chord. All groups sing simultaneously so the sound of the tonic chord can be audiated.

2. After a pause, Group 1 moves to the fifth of the subdominant chord, Group 2 moves to the root of the subdominant chord, and Group 3 moves to the third of the subdominant chord.

3. After a pause, Group 1 moves to the third of the dominant-seventh chord, Group 2 moves to the seventh of the dominant-seventh chord, and Group 3 moves to the root of the dominant-seventh chord.

4. After a pause, the groups move back to the tonic chord. Again, all of this is done through audiation and without notation. The chord progression tonic/subdominant/dominant-seventh/tonic in harmonic minor tonality is notated below.

5. All students as a group move their bodies to macrobeats. This is repeated until they feel comfortable audiating a span of eight macrobeats.

6. Now the students as a group sing the roots **using tonal syllables first and then neutral syllables** to the tonic/subdominant/

dominant-seventh/tonic chords in harmonic minor tonality over eight underlying macrobeats as notated below.

La　　Re　　Mi　　La

7. After you demonstrate in a comfortable singing range how to improvise melodic patterns, all students singing together using **neutral syllables** improvise their individual melodies to the familiar chord progression. The melodies may incorporate macrobeats, microbeats, divisions, and elongations. For the first two underlying macrobeats, the melody is based on only **harmonic minor tonic** pattern pitches; for the third and fourth underlying macrobeats, the melody is based on only **harmonic minor subdominant** pattern pitches; for the fifth and sixth underlying macrobeats, the melody is based on only **harmonic minor dominant-seventh** pattern pitches; and for the seventh and eight underlying macrobeats, the melody is based on only **harmonic minor tonic** pattern pitches. **No non-harmonic tones are used at this time.** When the performance of the ensemble sounds consonant, you know that all students are singing acceptable pitches.

8. As the class sings the chord progression of harmonic minor tonic/subdominant/dominant-seventh/tonic over eight underlying macrobeats, individual students take turns improvising a solo melody. Examples of appropriate individual students' improvisations are notated below.

PART SEVEN: HARMONIC IMPROVISATION - A

9. Before moving on, the groups change parts singing the chords.

Section H – Harmonic Minor: Tonic/Dominant-Seventh/Subdominant/Tonic

Student participation begins as outlined by step in the following sequential manner:

1. The class is divided into three groups of students. **Using tonal syllables first and then neutral syllables**, in harmonic minor tonality, Group 1 sings the root of the tonic chord, Group 2 sings the third of the tonic chord, and Group 3 sings the fifth of the tonic chord. All groups sing simultaneously so that the sound of the tonic chord can be audiated.

2. After a pause, Group 1 moves to the third of the dominant-seventh chord, Group 2 moves to the seventh of the dominant-seventh chord, and Group 3 moves to the root of the dominant-seventh chord.

3. After a pause, Group 1 moves to the fifth of the subdominant chord, Group 2 moves to the root of the subdominant chord, and Group 3 moves to the third of the subdominant chord.

4. After a pause, the groups move back to the tonic chord. Again, all of this is done through audiation and without notation. The chord progression tonic/dominant-seventh/

subdominant/tonic in harmonic minor tonality is notated below.

5. All students as a group move their bodies to macrobeats. This is repeated until they feel comfortable auditing a span of eight macrobeats.

6. Now the students as a group sing the roots **using tonal syllables first and then neutral syllables** to the tonic/dominant-seventh/subdominant/tonic chords in harmonic minor tonality over eight underlying macrobeats as notated below.

7. After you demonstrate in a comfortable singing range how to improvise melodic patterns, all students singing together using **neutral syllables** improvise their individual melodies to the familiar chord progression. The melodies may incorporate macrobeats, microbeats, divisions, and elongations. For the first two underlying macrobeats, the melody is based on only **harmonic minor tonic** pattern pitches; for the third and fourth underlying macrobeats, the melody is based on only **harmonic minor dominant-seventh** pattern pitches; for the fifth and sixth underlying macrobeats, the melody is based on only **harmonic minor subdominant** pattern pitches; and for the seventh and eight underlying macrobeats, the melody is based on only **harmonic minor tonic** pattern pitches. **No non-harmonic tones are used at this time.** When the performance of the ensemble sounds consonant, you know that all students are singing acceptable pitches.

8. As the class sings the chord progression of harmonic minor tonic/dominant-seventh/subdominant/tonic over eight underlying macrobeats, individual students take turns improvising a solo melody. Examples of appropriate individual students' improvisations are notated below.

9. Before moving on, the groups change parts singing the chords.

Part Eight
Harmonic Improvisation - B

The students will now be improvising melodies over chord progressions based upon **eight** underlying macrobeats using **neutral syllables**. However, non-harmonic tones (pitches not included in the chord), rests, and upbeats may also be included in the improvisations along with macrobeats, microbeats, divisions, and elongations.

Tonality and keyality and the meter and tempo in which the harmonic patterns are to be audiated should be established before teaching students to improvise melodies over harmonic progressions. Although the majority of examples in this part of the book are in usual duple meter, they may serve as models for improvising in other meters, as shown at the end.

It must be emphasized to students that as they are singing non-harmonic tones, they must at the same time be audiating the sonance of each underlying chord in the chord progression.

Dissonance is a natural result of the use of non-harmonic tones. Students should not be advised to avoid discord, but rather, to use it discerningly. An artistic resolution of dissonance should be anticipated in audiation.

Section A – Major: Tonic/Subdominant/ Dominant-Seventh/ Tonic

1. The chord progressions (and chord roots if warranted) may be reviewed by students singing them using **neutral syllables**. When necessary, however, tonal syllables may be revisited to clarify audiation uncertainties. Changing parts often is

recommended. The chord progression and chord roots tonic/subdominant/dominant-seventh/tonic are notated below.

2. As the class sings the chord progression of major tonic/subdominant/dominant-seventh/tonic over eight underlying macrobeats, individual students take turns improvising a solo melody. For the first two underlying macrobeats, the melody is based on the tonic chord; for the third and fourth underlying macrobeats, the melody is based on the subdominant chord; for the fifth and sixth macrobeats, the melody is based on the dominant-seventh chord; and for the seventh and eighth underlying macrobeats, the melody is based on the tonic chord. Below are examples of appropriate individual students' improvisations in various keyalities.

Section B – Major: Tonic/Dominant-Seventh/Subdominant/Tonic

1. The chord progressions (and chord roots if warranted) may be reviewed by students singing them using **neutral syllables**.

Part Eight: Harmonic Improvisation - B

When necessary, however, tonal syllables may be revisited to clarify audiation uncertainties. Changing parts often is recommended. The chord progression and chord roots tonic/dominant-seventh/subdominant/tonic are notated below.

2. As the class sings the chord progression of major tonic/dominant-seventh/subdominant tonic over eight underlying macrobeats, individual students take turns improvising a solo melody. For the first two underlying macrobeats, the melody is based on the tonic chord; for the third and fourth underlying macrobeats, the melody is based on the dominant-seventh chord; for the fifth and sixth macrobeats, the melody is based on the subdominant chord; and for the seventh and eighth underlying macrobeats, the melody is based on the tonic chord. Below are examples of appropriate individual students' improvisations in various keyalities.

Section C – Harmonic Minor: Tonic/Subdominant/Dominant-Seventh/Tonic

1. The chord progressions (and chord roots if warranted) may be reviewed by students singing them using **neutral syllables.** When necessary, however, tonal syllables may be revisited to clarify audiation uncertainties. Changing parts often is recommended. The chord progression and chord roots tonic/subdominant/dominant-seventh/tonic are notated below.

2. As the class sings the chord progression of harmonic minor tonic/subdominant/dominant-seventh/tonic over eight underlying macrobeats, individual students take turns improvising a solo melody. For the first two underlying macrobeats, the melody is based on the tonic chord; for the third and fourth underlying macrobeats, the melody is based on the subdominant chord; for the fifth and sixth macrobeats, the melody is based on the dominant-seventh chord; and for the seventh and eighth underlying macrobeats, the melody is based on the tonic chord. Below are examples of appropriate individual students' improvisations in various keyalities.

Section D – Harmonic Minor: Tonic/Dominant-Seventh/Subdominant/Tonic

1. The chord progressions (and chord roots if warranted) may be reviewed by students singing them using **neutral syllables.** When necessary, however, tonal syllables may be revisited to clarify audiation uncertainties. Changing parts often is recommended. The chord progression and chord roots tonic/dominant-seventh/subdominant/tonic are notated below.

2. As the class sings the chord progression of harmonic minor tonic/dominant-seventh/subdominant/tonic over eight underlying macrobeats, individual students take turns improvising a solo melody. For the first two underlying macrobeats, the melody is based on the tonic chord; for the third and fourth underlying macrobeats, the melody is based on the dominant-seventh chord; for the fifth and sixth macrobeats, the melody is based on the subdominant chord; and for the seventh and eighth underlying macrobeats, the melody is based on the tonic chord. Below are examples of appropriate individual students' improvisations in various keyalities.

Before moving on to examples of improvisations in major and harmonic minor tonalities in usual triple and usual combined meters, the following challenging activities might be pursued.

1. Small groups of students, taking turns, may hold up fingers indicating appropriate chord changes as the class sings familiar songs.

2. Individual students may hold up fingers indicating appropriate chord changes as the class sings familiar songs.

3. While explaining to students that no one chord is always the "absolute correct" one when harmonizing a melody, offer options that might be used as substitutions for the chord agreed upon by the class. Contrasting chords that share common pitches offer the best opportunity to underscore the concept. The class might actually sing the chords and compare their suitability. Above all, emphasize that in improvisation, there are no mistakes, only improper inartistic solutions, and that dissonance often proves to be desirable and artistic.

4. Assign students out-of-school activities. For example, they may be asked to discover which familiar songs incorporate only the I and V7 chords or include the II7 chord.

Section E - Usual Triple and Usual Combined Meters

Below are notated examples of improvisations in usual triple meter and usual combined meter imposed on eight underlying macrobeats. They are based on major and harmonic minor implied tonic, dominant-seventh, and subdominant chord progressions in a variety of keyalities (non-harmonic tones included). Macrobeats, microbeats, divisions, elongations, rests, and upbeats are found throughout. Chords symbols indicating implied harmony are above the melody.

Part Eight: Harmonic Improvisation - B

Part Nine

Advanced Harmonic Improvisation - A

Once students are comfortable improvising in major and harmonic minor tonalities using the three fundamental chords combined with non-harmonic tones and with various types of rhythm patterns in more than one meter, they are ready to engage in longer improvisations that incorporate additional chords. Only major tonality in the three already familiar usual meters of duple, triple, and combined will be discussed.

With advanced instruction in improvisation, individual musical differences among students becomes pronounced. Most obvious in the improvisation process is that some students are capable of predicting chord changes, others are able to react only to chord changes, and others seem to oblivious to chord changes. Thus, the same guidance for all students in a group is not the best procedure. Rather, instruction is best adapted to students' individual musical needs as determined by their readiness to participate in advanced group improvisation.

It would be prudent to administer two types of tests to students before proceeding with improvisation activities. The first type should be one of music aptitude. For students in upper elementary and middle schools, the *Intermediate Measures of Music Audiation* (IMMA) is appropriate. For older students, the *Advanced Measures of Music Audiation* (AMMA) is recommended. The interpretation of results for both tests is as follows: scores at or above the 80th percentile are high, scores between the 21st and 79th percentile are average, and scores at or below the 20th percentile are low.

Because music aptitude is a measure of one's potential to learn music, and students differ greatly in this regard, be prepared to take time and be patient with less-able students in the group, providing repetition as often as needed, while allowing and encouraging more-able students to move ahead more quickly. This may be accomplished without making students feel inferior or vain when instruction is directed properly to enhance the potential of all students in the group. Group instruction is a must, because students learn a great deal from one another. Procedures for adapting instruction to students' musical strengths and weaknesses are explained in each test manual.

The second type of test is one that focuses specifically on improvisation. It is the *Harmonic Improvisation Readiness Record* (HIRR). Results on the test quickly indicate the level of each student's readiness to engage in improvisation activities. Given this objective information before instruction is undertaken, a teacher need not waste valuable class time in attempting to subjectively uncover this important knowledge. Thus, quality of instruction is raised to a high level and students' attitudes remain positive when objective information is combined with subjective wisdom. A companion test, the *Rhythm Improvisation Readiness Record* (RIRR), which is composed of time patterns (not rhythm patterns) may be administered along with HIRR to discover the extent to which students act or react to chord changes. All of these tests are published by GIA.

Adapting Instruction to Students' Harmonic Improvisation Readiness

Results on the *Harmonic Improvisation Readiness Record* are used to arrange a class into two groups. The students are not physically separated or put into different sections. Rather, all students, regardless of how they score on HIRR, are best taught together in one group in the same classroom.

Scores on the *Harmonic Improvisation Readiness Record* are given serious attention to determine whether students are ready to profit from participation in activities associated especially with advanced improvisation. How well students achieved in preliminary improvisation activities outlined in previous parts of this book is of course important, but for their further development, that should be considered of secondary importance at this time. Thus, depending upon their HIRR results, the suggested relevant guidelines should be taken into account in the instructional setting, even if some aspects appear to be a repeat or re-enforcement of what students, particularly those with typical readiness, might have already experienced.

Students With Little Or No Readiness

Listening and learning to audiate is of primary importance for students who lack readiness to learn to participate in advanced harmonic improvisation. Listening should be informal, in and out of school, and is best directed by the teacher. A student cannot listen too much. Music in which harmonic patterns are simple and obvious is best. All styles of music should be heard, although music with pronounced rhythm and sensitive tone quality, not unnecessarily loud or overly repetitious, provides the most advantageous background.

Students might best begin to perform in terms of movement, not dance. They may move their legs and arms, not hands and fingers, with continuous and flowing movement in place or around the room, preferably without music in the background. No beat should be audible as the students are moving. With that accomplished, students may respond to a beat with a pulsating wrist movement combined with their continuous and flowing movement. Music still should not be used. The beat is established by the teacher demonstrating or chanting softly.

After students feel comfortable with their bodies and can move expressively in a consistent tempo, they may begin to sing chord roots in accompaniment to songs that include only tonic and dominant-seventh chords, and later songs that include only tonic, dominant-seventh, and subdominant chords. Songs in only major and harmonic minor tonalities should be used, and as many songs in harmonic minor tonality as in major tonality should be performed. Students learn best by making comparisons. They do not learn what something is, they learn what it is not by comparing it to something else. That is why the perpetual use of only the tonic chord in major tonality will probably prove to be of little benefit, and perhaps some harm. And, to keep using only one meter is equally undesirable. Music that students hear and perform should be in as many meters as possible.

Students With Typical and Superior Readiness

Notated below is the same taxonomy of harmonic patterns in major and harmonic minor tonalities presented in part six but now arranged according to the difficulty levels of easy, moderately difficult, and difficult. The reports of the research in categorizing the harmonic patterns can be found in Edwin E. Gordon, *Manual* for the *Harmonic Improvisation Readiness Record and Rhythm Improvisation Readiness Record,* Chicago: GIA, 1998 and Edwin E. Gordon, *Studies in Harmonic and Rhythmic Improvisation Readiness,* Chicago: GIA, 2000.

As explained in part six, these three-chord patterns begin and end with the tonic chord. For purposes of enrichment and remedial or compensatory instruction, students may be introduced to specific harmonic patterns incorporated into their improvisations in accordance with their HIRR scores, their demonstrated achievement and aspirations, and the judgment of the teacher. The difficult patterns are particularly suited to high-scoring students, the moderately-difficult patterns to average-scoring students, and the easy

PART NINE: ADVANCED HARMONIC IMPROVISATION - A

patterns to low-scoring students. Whether or not patterns in the taxonomy are used, it is important to understand that for customary instruction, the procedures outlined on the following pages should be considered primary and indispensable to ensure the proper sequential progress of students with typical and superior readiness.

EASY

Major

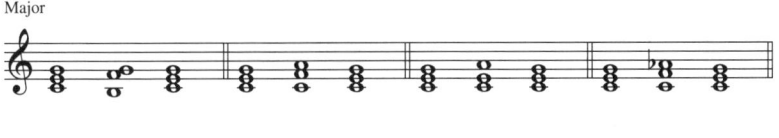

Harmonic Minor

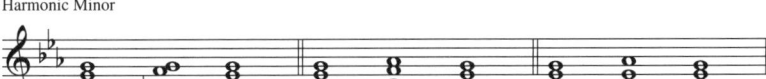

MODERATELY DIFFICULT

Major

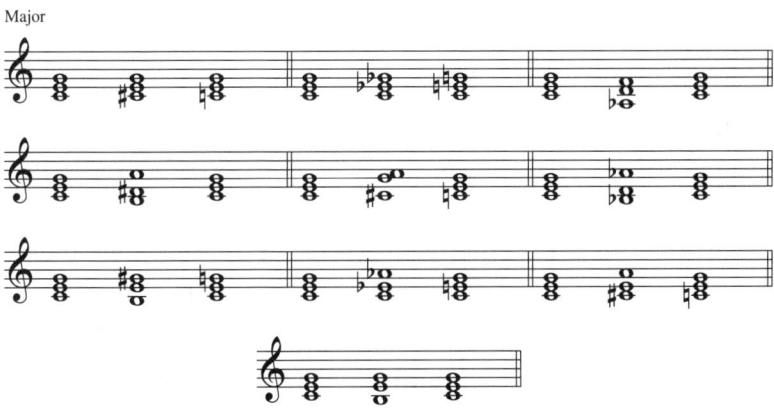

Harmonic Minor

DIFFICULT

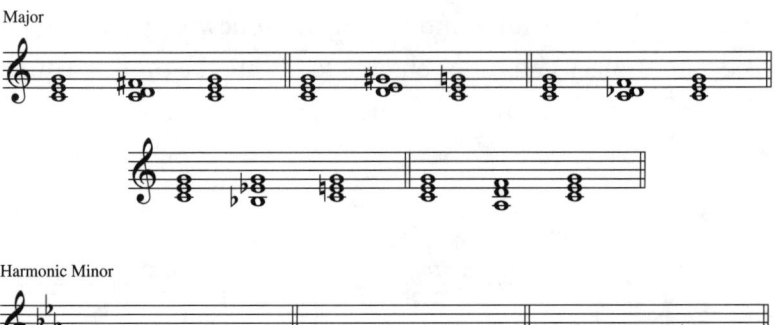

Major

Harmonic Minor

There are six chords in major tonality that provide the foundation for advanced improvisation when audiated in the three usual meters. They are the II7, VI7, and III7 in major tonality. They are best learned sequentially in the order above, not all at once.

All three chords are major-minor seventh-chords, that is, the lower part is a major triad and the upper part includes the minor seventh pitch. (That has been the case for the V7 chord that students have been performing thus far.) For example, in the keyality of C, the II7 chord is spelled D F# A C; the VI7, A C# E G; and the III7, E G# B D. It is important that the chords initially be presented as major-minor sevenths rather than as minor-minor sevenths (for example, D F A C), as is often found in jazz. When audiated and performed as major-minor sevenths, the third of the chord contributes to the further contextual development of a strong sense of tonality, because of the chord's natural sequential resolution to the tonic.

Conspicuous by its absence is the IV chord. Although it played an important role in earlier improvisations, for the time being its function is replaced by the II7 chord. Later, the IV chord will come into use again, and so will the IV7 chord when it leads to a modulation. That is not the case with the I7 chord, which will be used subsequently in resolution to the IV chord.

When students perform improvisations over a chord progression that includes one of the three major-minor seventh-chords, it is recommended that they not include the chromatic alterations in the melody. If, however, some students do alter the melody, particularly high-scoring students on the tests, they should not be discouraged from doing so. Melodic chromaticism, nonetheless, will be approached by the entire class at a later time.

Before using the three major-minor seventh-chords in improvisation, the class in unison should imitate the teacher's singing of only chord roots using **tonal syllables first and then neutral syllables**, each chord being named by the students. The notation for this is found below for progressions including the three major-minor seventh-chords. For ease of identification, chord symbols are included above the notation. Improvisation using the complete chords as a foundation is initiated after the students are comfortable audiating chord roots.

After a short review of improvising using the I, IV, and V7 chords in major tonality, the class may begin to sing **and name** the II7 chord in a progression in major tonality using **tonal syllables first and then neutral syllables**. Notice in the notation below that there are only three pitches in all chords, the fifth of the chord being excluded. (Remember, that was the principle for the V7 chord used in all previous work.) With the class, as before, being sectioned into three groups, the chord progression is sung in unison and each chord is named by the students. Time might be allowed so that the students may have the opportunity to sing each part of all chords.

As the class sings the chord progression of I II7 V7 I using **neutral syllables**, individual students take turns improvising a solo melody over eight underlying macrobeats using **neutral syllables**. Examples of student's improvisations that the teacher might demonstrate are notated below with chord symbols identifying implied harmony. It is expected that the judicious use of non-harmonic tones will play a prominent role in the improvisations, particularly those of high-scoring students on the tests.

The VI7 chord in major tonality may now be sung **and named** in a chord progression. The progression notated below is best sung in unison using **tonal syllables first and then neutral syllables**. All students should be given the opportunity to sing each part of all chords.

PART NINE: ADVANCED HARMONIC IMPROVISATION - A   101

As the class sings the chord progression of I VI7 II7 V7 I using **neutral syllables**, individual students take turns improvising a solo melody over eight underlying macrobeats using **neutral syllables**. Because there are only eight underlying macrobeats, some familiar chord changes occur from one macrobeat to the other. Thus it may be prudent initially to establish a slower tempo for the chord progression. As seen, the introduction of the new chord, VI7, is extended over two underlying macrobeats.

Examples of students' improvisations that the teacher might demonstrate are notated below with chord symbols identifying implied harmony. It should be expected that non-harmonic tones will become more prevalent as new chords are added to the progression.

The III7 chord in major tonality may now be sung **and named** in a chord progression. The progression notated below is best sung in unison using **tonal syllables and then neutral syllables**. All students should be given the opportunity to sing each part of all chords.

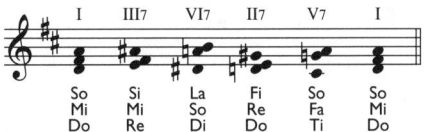

As the class sings the chord progression of I III7 VI7 II7 V7 I using **neutral syllables**, individual students take turns improvising a solo melody over eight underlying macrobeats using **neutral syllables**. Again, because there are only eight underlying macrobeats, some familiar chord changes occur from one macrobeat to the other. Thus it may be prudent initially to establish a slower tempo for the chord progression. As seen, the introduction of the new chord, III7, is extended over two underlying macrobeats.

Examples of students' improvisations that the teacher might demonstrate are notated below with chord symbols identifying implied harmony. It should be expected that non-harmonic tones will become more prevalent as new chords are added to the progression.

Whenever it appears advantageous, the following techniques, some familiar and others unfamiliar, might be reviewed and introduced.

1. Improvise or sing familiar major songs that include only the I and V7 chords. As the song is being sung, hold up fingers to indicate to students an appropriate chord that goes with the melody.

2. Next, after establishing eight underlying macrobeats, hold up

fingers to indicate the I or V7 chord in major tonality. All students together improvise a melody based on the progression. Then individual students take turns improvising a melody for the same or different progressions of the I and V7 chords. Be clear: The chords are not sung by the class during individual improvisations. The students are expected to audiate the chord changes as they observe the teacher's finger changes. You may need to perform several improvisations while changing fingers to assist students in understanding the procedure.

3. Individual students in front of the class may take turns holding up fingers as all students together improvise a melody based on the indicated chord progression. Students may be relieved of constraints by the teacher emphasizing that when improvising, there are no mistakes, only improper solutions.

4. Follow Steps 1, 2, and 3 using a I-IV-V7-I progression in major tonality.

5. Follow Steps 1, 2, and 3 using a I-II7-V7-I progression in major tonality. At this time and forward, additional underlying macrobeats may be added to the progression.

6. Follow Steps 1, 2, and 3 using a I-VI7-II7-V7-I progression in major tonality.

7. Follow Steps 1, 2, and 3 using a I-III7-VI7-II7-V7-I progression in major tonality.

Part Ten

Advanced Harmonic Improvisation - B

Now that students are able to audiate the six fundamental chords and improvise melodies based on progressions that include them, they have demonstrated their ability to audiate harmonically the altered tones in the third of the II7, VI7, and III7 chords while improvising melodies. **Now they are prepared to use chromatic tones in addition to other non-harmonic tones in melodic improvisations that may or may not coincide with the altered tones in the six chords as well as in the I7 chord and beyond. Further, a chord progression need no longer follow familiar schemes.** That is, the V7 may resolve to a chord other than I, the V7 may resolve to the IV, the III7 may resolve directly to IV, II7 or V7, and so on. Examples of various types of improvisations based on some of the progressions described above are notated below. **Improvisations for a given progression need not be restricted to a specific number of underlying macrobeats, and some chords may change for consecutive macrobeats.** The specifications for a given progression, however, must be explained to students before improvisations are initiated.

Part Ten: Advanced Harmonic Improvisation - B

Part Eleven

Advanced Harmonic Improvisation - C

When an improvisation is prepared momentarily before it is actually performed, audiation is taking place. Without preliminary audiation, there can be only capricious exploration, even though it might be called improvisation. When students, regardless of their chronological age or traditional formal music instruction, have phased through the heretofore improvisation essentials, they are able to audiate sufficiently to undertake the following improvisation ventures. Patience, however, is necessary on the part of the teacher as well as the students. Pause to provide students time to audiate the specific chord progression that they will be using as the basis for their improvisations. As the class audiates macrobeats and sings the chord progression, you might perform an improvisation over that progression as an example.

It will be necessary for you to establish a consistent system of finger gestures so that students will know what they are to audiate. For example, for the I chord, one finger might be raised; for the IV chord, four fingers raised; for the V7 chord, five fingers raised; and for the VI7 chord, both hands used to raise six fingers. To expand this, the teacher might point fingers downward to indicate that the chord is a minor-minor seventh rather than a major-minor seventh. Also, for the minor IV chord, all four fingers may be pointed downward, or only one finger on the alternate hand might be directed downward. For the I7 chord, one finger of one hand may go up and one finger on the hand down. The crucial issue is that whatever system is selected, it must be used consistently.

Below are examples of improvisations based on chord progressions that include minor-minor seventh-chords. The small *m* included in the chord symbol for a seventh chord indicates that it is minor-minor, and the small *m* associated with the IV chord indicates that it is a minor chord. These chords are often found in all types of popular music, jazz notwithstanding.

For more extended types of improvisations, it is good to begin with the "twelve-bar" blues. If the progression is not familiar to students, play recorded performances of some jazz renditions, new and old, so that students will become comfortable with the sound and find it effortless to audiate. Below are two chord progressions that outline the blues. The first is the simpler of the two. The second is easily audiated as a modification of the first. The notes in the measures are not pitches, they indicate only the length of each chord. The blues are typically performed in a variety of keyalities.

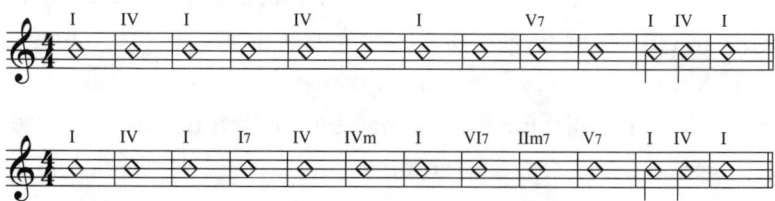

An example of a melody that obligates a longer chord progression is notated below. Although it is only sixteen measures long, it may be considered an incipient popular tune.

At this time, it may prove advantageous for students to investigate the possibilities modulations have to offer in improvisation. In the beginning, the changes of keyalities should be simple. For example, they might move to the dominant and subdominant keyalities of the original keyality as notated below. Both examples are in major tonality and begin in the keyality of C. The first one moves to G and back again, and the second moves to F and back again. In the notation, the chord symbols in parenthesis are in the changed keyality. New finger and/or hand gestures will be required to indicate modulations.

Later on, after students have been introduced to improvisations in harmonic minor tonality, they should find it attractive to modulate back and forth between major and minor tonalities as well as between different keyalities.

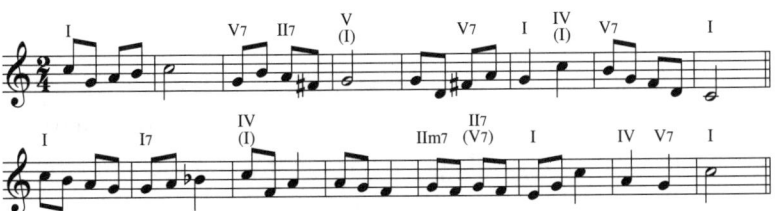

I have found that improvising in tonalities other than major and harmonic minor provides for expansive audiation as well as for delightful musical experiences. Below are noted the fundamental chords for Dorian, Phrygian, Lydian, Mixolydian, and Aeolian tonalities. The same procedures for introducing students to improvisation in major tonality are used for improvising in the less-familiar tonalities. Notice in the notation that only triads are used, not seventh chords, and that the VII chord is a subtonic chord. The subtonic is a whole step below the tonic. Of course, as before, keyalities that accommodate the range and tessitura of the students should be used. Remember, for example, just as C is the relative minor of Eb major, F is the relative Dorian Eb major, G is the relative Phrygian of Eb major, Ab is the relative Lydian of Eb major, and Bb is the relative Mixolydian of Eb major.

Before moving on to part twelve and explaining the transition of vocal improvisation to instrumental improvisation, a few concluding comments seem in order. Needless to say, vocal improvisations based on previously used chord progressions are advantageously undertaken in usual triple and usual combined meters, as well as with unusual meters. In usual meters, the macrobeats are of equal length. In unusual meters, the macrobeat are not of equal length, but the microbeats are of equal length. For example, in 5/8 (all five eighth-notes are microbeats), one macrobeat is the length of a quarter note and the other macrobeat is the length of a dotted-quarter note. In 7/8, (all seven eighth-notes are microbeats), two macrobeats are the length of a quarter note and the remaining macrobeat is the length of a dotted-quarter note. In 8/8, (all eight eighth-notes are microbeats), two macrobeats are the length of a dotted-quarter note and the remaining macrobeat is the length of a quarter note. However, whatever meter is to be performed, it must be established before improvisations are begun by students audiating and moving their bodies using their legs and arms simultaneously to ascertain the identity of macrobeats and microbeats.

Finally, the chord progressions of typical popular tunes that extend for 32 measures might be learned and audiated as students improvise new melodies above the chord progression as a modification or adaptation of the original one, or even a substitution for the composer's intent. If need be, students may begin by performing a simple melodic variation of the original melody as a prelude to harmonic improvisation. The songs may be performed in a jazz style, as professional musicians do, with or without text or just by scat singing. And those so inclined might avail themselves to country and blue-grass music, both genres offering enormous possibilities for improvisation. The chord progressions are comparatively less complicated than those associated with popular tunes that emanate from musicals, and for the most part, they are inventive in a unique artistic manner.

Part Twelve

Making the Transition from Voice to Instruments

As a result of being familiar with tonal solfege and terminology such as *tonic, dominant, macrobeat,* and *microbeat,* students are now well prepared to transfer easily and with confidence their vocal improvisations skills to instrumental improvisation. Although the steps outlined below are for only major tonality and usual duple meter, they set the procedure for improvising instrumentally in other tonalities and meters.

1. Review using **tonal syllables** the singing of the tonic, dominant-seventh, and subdominant chords in major tonality. Notice the notation below. The chords are in different inversions from the positions in which students have previously performed them. The reason for the change is because the three chords in the new positions are easier to play on the recorder, the instrument that will be used to explain the transition to instrumental improvisation.

2. Before they begin playing the recorder, the class is divided into three groups to sing using **tonal syllables** the chords as notated. No improvisations are necessary to audiate the sonance of the chords.

3. After you establish major tonality in the keyality of *C* for the class, all students sing *do* together. Then show the students where to place their fingers on the recorder to produce *C-do* in the upper octave. The students as a group play *C-do*.

4. Chant using rhythm syllables a rhythm pattern in usual duple meter four macrobeats in length. The students imitate the pattern vocally.

5. Placing their fingers for *C-do* on the recorder, students play the rhythm pattern. No pitch other than *C* is used.

6. Chant additional rhythm patterns, and the students imitate them on the recorder on *C-do*. You may sometimes play the rhythm patterns on the recorder for students to imitate.

7. Show students where to place their fingers for *re* in the lower octave. **Do not call it *D-re*.** Simply refer to it as *re*.

8. Sing using **neutral syllables** or play some rhythm patterns on the recorder that include both pitches. If the recorder is used, students should not see your fingerings. They must audiate the changes of pitch. Either stand behind the students or turn your back to them so they do not see your fingers moving.

9. Show students where to place their fingers for *mi* in the lower octave. **Do not call it *E-mi*.** Simply refer to it as *mi*.

10. Sing using **neutral syllables** or play some rhythm patterns on the recorder that include all three pitches. Again, If the recorder is used, students should not see your fingerings. They must audiate the changes of pitch.

11. Show students where to place their fingers for *ti* below *do*. **Do not call it *B-ti*.** Simply refer to it as *ti*.

12. Sing using **neutral syllables** or play some rhythm patterns on the recorder that include all four pitches. Remember, if the recorder is used, students must not see your fingerings. They need to audiate the changes of pitch.

Chapter Twelve: Making the Transition from Voice to Instruments

Students are now ready to begin initial harmonic improvisation on the recorder. No notation should be used at this time. Later, after the content of this has been understood, notation might be used, particularly for reading chord symbols that indicate the harmonic foundation upon which improvisations are to be based.

1. The class is divided into three groups. Each group is to play on the recorder one pitch of each of the three chords.

2. Look at the notation below to see again the new positions of the tonic, dominant-seventh, and subdominant chords.

3. Show students in each group how to finger their pitch for the tonic chord. Students play the tonic chord on the recorder. Tell them it is the tonic chord.

4. Show students in each group how to finger their pitch for the dominant-seventh chord. Students play the dominant-seventh chord on the recorder. Tell them it is the dominant-seventh chord.

5. Show students in each group how to finger their pitch for the subdominant chord. Students play the subdominant chord on the recorder. Tell them it is the subdominant chord.

6. Explain to students which fingers of your's symbolize each chord. Then hold up fingers to indicate which chord is to be played as students as an ensemble play various progressions that include the three chords.

7. Establish a chord progression beginning and ending with the tonic chord. Each chord is sustained the length of two macrobeats, eight macrobeats in all.

8. Students take turns improvising on the recorder a melody over the chord progression. Only four pitches are to be used: *do, re, mi, ti.*

9. Teach all students how to finger and play *fa, so, la,* and low *do.*

10. Now students improvise using all eight pitches of the *C* scale, each chord being sustained for two macrobeats, eight macrobeats in all.

Students are now ready to begin advanced harmonic improvisation on the recorder.

1. To play the II7, VI7, and III7 chords, students will need to learn fingerings for three chromatic pitches, essentially F#, C#, and G#. The positions for the chords are notated below. The fingerings for additional chromatics are taught as the need arises to fulfill the audiation of students' further melodic and chordal improvisations.

2. Students are now prepared to improvise over a progression in which some chords are sustained for only one macrobeat. That does not necessarily require that improvisations be longer than eight macrobeats. However, improvisations based on sixteen or more macrobeats are actually easier to audiate and perform when chord changes are more frequent.

3. Before teaching students to improvise in keyalities other than *C,* they should begin to improvise in usual triple and combined meters and, if befitting, in unusual meters.

4. It is beneficial for students to learn to improvise in different tonalities before they improvise in a variety of keyalities in major tonality. Harmonic minor tonality in the keyality of *A* (the resting tone changing from *do* to *la*) is the logical choice to initiate the venture. Students are already familiar with the fingering for G#. The chords for *A-la* are notated below.

5. As with vocal improvisation, students should change parts often when performing chords instrumentally.

6. There will be students who desire to improvise on instruments apart from the recorder. If that be the case, they should do so in ensembles with heterogeneous instrumentation, including students who represent a variety of music aptitude and harmonic improvisation readiness levels. Students with variable backgrounds learn a great deal from one another.

7. When and if students begin to read music notation in their improvisations, they will need to understand the chord symbols above the notation. They will quickly understand that when they see, for example, the chord symbols C, F, and G7, such nomenclature is a translation for indicating I, IV, and V7.

Glossary

Aeolian Tonality — The tonality of "la" to "la" with "la" as the resting tone. When compared to harmonic minor tonality, it has a lowered seventh step.

Arpeggiated Pattern — A tonal pattern in which almost all of the pitches move by skip, not by step.

Audiation — Hearing and comprehending in one's mind the sound of music that is not or may never have been physically present. It is neither imitation nor memorization. There are six stages of audiation and eight types of audiation.

Content — Tonal patterns and rhythm patterns that constitute a piece of music.

Context — The tonality and meter of a piece of music that comprises the component parts of a piece of music.

Creativity — The spontaneous audiation and use of tonal patterns and rhythm patterns without restrictions.

Developmental Music Aptitude — Music potential that is affected by the quality of environmental factors. A child is in the developmental music aptitude stage from birth to approximately nine years old.

Diatonic — Music that moves by half steps and whole steps but does not include chromatic pitches.

Division Pattern — One function of rhythm patterns. A division pattern includes a division of a microbeat (a duration shorter than a microbeat) or a division

Glossary

	of a macrobeat (a duration shorter than a macrobeat but not a microbeat).
Division/Elongation Pattern	One function of rhythm patterns. A division/elongation pattern includes an elongation of a microbeat (a duration longer than a microbeat but not a macrobeat) and/or an elongation of a macrobeat (a duration longer than a macrobeat) or a division of a microbeat (a duration shorter than a microbeat) and/or a division of a macrobeat (a duration shorter than a macrobeat but not a microbeat).
"Do" Signature	That which is traditionally called a key signature. It does not, however, indicate any one tonality or keyality. It does indicate where "do" is found on the staff.
Dominant Pattern	One function of tonal patterns. A dominant (dominant-seventh) pattern in major tonality, for example, includes an arrangement of the tonal syllables "so ti re fa."
Dorian Tonality	The tonality of "re" to "re" with "re" as the resting tone. When compared to harmonic minor tonality, it has a raised sixth step and a lowered seventh step.
Duple Meter	See usual duple meter.
Duration	A part of a rhythm pattern. For example, each eighth note in a rhythm pattern of two eighth-notes is a duration.
Elongation Pattern	One function of rhythm patterns. An elongation pattern includes an elongation of a microbeat (a duration longer than a microbeat but not a macrobeat) or an elongation of a macrobeat (a duration longer than a macrobeat).

Enharmonic	Two tonal patterns that sound the same but are notated differently. Also, two key signatures that are used to notate the same-sounding keyality.
Enrhythmic	Two rhythm patterns that sound the same but are notated differently. Also, two measure signatures that are used to notate the same-sounding meter. Enrhythmic is to rhythm notation and audiation what enharmonic is to tonal notation and audiation.
Harmonic Minor Tonality	The tonality of "la" to "la" with "la" as the resting tone. When compared to Aeolian tonality, it has a raised seventh step. Harmonic minor, not Aeolian, is a basic tonality in learning sequence activities. Melodic minor and both types of Hungarian (Gypsy) minor are variations of harmonic minor tonality.
Harmonic Pattern	Two or more chords that are audiated as a sonority in a linear sequential manner.
Harmonic Pattern Progression	Two or more harmonic patterns that are audiated as a sonority in a linear sequential manner.
Improvisation	The spontaneous audiation and use of tonal patterns and rhythm patterns with restrictions.
Intact Macrobeat	A macrobeat in unusual meter that is not long enough to be divided into microbeats. It can be divided only into divisions of a microbeat. An intact macrobeat is the durational equivalent of a microbeat.
Key Signature	That which is actually a "do" signature. A key signature is seen in notation, whereas a keyality is audiated. A key signature does not indicate any one keyality. For example, the key

GLOSSARY   123

                          signature of three flats may indicate Eb keyality in major tonality, C keyality in harmonic minor or Aeolian tonality, F keyality in Dorian tonality, G keyality in Phrygian tonality, Ab keyality in Lydian tonality, Bb keyality in Mixolydian tonality, and D keyality in Locrian tonality. Nevertheless, although "do" is not the resting tone in all of those tonalities, Eb is "do" in all of them.

Keyality   The pitch name of the tonic. A keyality is audiated, whereas a key signature is seen in notation. C is the keyality in C major, in C harmonic minor and Aeolian, in C Dorian, in C Phrygian, and so on. A tonic is associated with a keyality, whereas a resting tone is associated with a tonality.

Locrian Tonality   The tonality of "ti" to "ti" with "ti" as the resting tone. When compared to harmonic minor tonality, it has a lowered second step, a raised third step, a lowered fifth step, a raised sixth step, and a lowered seventh step.

Lydian Tonality   The tonality of "fa" to "fa" with "fa" as the resting tone. When compared to major tonality, it has a raised fourth step.

Macro/Microbeat Pattern   One function of rhythm patterns. A macro/microbeat pattern includes combinations of macrobeats and microbeats, only macrobeats, or only microbeats.

Macrobeats   The fundamental beats in a rhythm pattern. In usual duple meter with the measure signature 2/4, quarter notes are the performed or underlying macrobeats. In usual triple meter with the measure signature 6/8, dotted-quarter notes are the performed or underlying macrobeats. In usual triple meter with the measure signature 3/4, dotted-half notes are the performed or underlying macrobeats. In unusual meters with the measure signatures 5/8 and 7/8, the performed or underlying macrobeats are combinations of quarter notes and dotted-quarter notes.

Major-Minor Seventh-Chord	The lower tetrachord is major and the upper tetrachord is minor. For example, D F# A C.
Minor-Minor Seventh-Chords	Both the lower and upper tetrachords are minor. For example, D F A C.
Major Tonality	The tonality of "do" to "do" with "do" as the resting tone. When compared to harmonic minor tonality, it has a raised third step and a raised sixth step.
Measure Signature	Traditionally called a time signature or a meter signature. A measure signature, however, indicates neither meter nor time. It indicates only the fractional value of a whole note that will be found in a measure. Because measure signatures are enrhythmic, a measure signature cannot indicate any one meter. Tempo markings and metronome markings indicate tempo, measure signatures do not.
Melodic Pattern	The combining of a tonal pattern and a rhythm pattern.
Memorization	Repeating without the use of notated music that was read or heard, but not necessarily audiated.
Meter	Usual meter is determined by how macrobeats of equal length are divided. There are three types of usual meter. When macrobeats are divided into two microbeats of equal duration,

Glossary

the result is usual duple meter. When macrobeats are divided into three microbeats of equal duration, the result is usual triple meter. When some macrobeats are divided into two microbeats and others are divided into three microbeats, and not all of the microbeats are of equal duration, the result is usual combined meter. Unusual meter is determined by how macrobeats of unequal temporal lengths, some of which may be intact, are grouped. There are four types of unusual meter. They are unusual paired, unusual unpaired, unusual paired intact, and unusual unpaired intact.

Microbeats — The equal divisions of a macrobeat. The following are examples. In usual duple meter with the measure signature 2/4, groups of two eighth-notes are the performed or underlying microbeats. In usual triple meter with the measure signature 6/8, groups of three eighth-notes are the performed or underlying microbeats, or in usual triple meter with the measure signature 3/4, groups of three quarter-notes are the performed or underlying microbeats. In unusual meters with the measure signatures 5/8 and 7/8, groups of two eighth-notes and groups of three eighth notes are the performed or underlying microbeats.

Minor Tonality — See harmonic minor tonality.

Mixolydian Tonality — The tonality of "so" to "so" with "so" as the resting tone. When compared to major tonality, it has a lowered seventh step.

Movable "do" Syllables — The tonal system in which the placement and position of "do" are dependent on keyality. For example, in major tonality, C is "do" in the keyality of C; D is "do" in the keyality of D; and so on. The ascending chromatic syllables are "do, di, re, ri, mi, fa, fi, so, si, la, li, ti, and do." The descending chromatic syllables are "do, ti, te, la, le, so, se, fa, mi, me, re, ra, and do." In the immovable or fixed "do" system, regardless of keyality, C is always "do." The tonal syllable system that is used in learning sequence activities is movable "do" with a "la" based minor.

Music Achievement	Accomplishment in music.
Music Aptitude	The potential to achieve in music.
Music Learning Theory	The analysis and synthesis of the sequential manner in which we learn when we learn music.
Neutral Syllable	A nonsense syllable, rather than tonal syllables or rhythm syllables, used to perform a pattern.
Notational Audiation	The audiation of what is seen in music notation without the aid of physical sound.
Note	A symbol that is read or written in music notation and represents what is being audiated.
Objective Keyality	A keyality for which there is consensus.
Objective Meter	A meter for which there is consensus.
Objective Tempo	A tempo for which there is consensus.
Objective Tonality	A tonality for which there is consensus.
Phrygian Tonality	The tonality of "mi" to "mi" with "mi" as the resting tone. When compared to harmonic minor tonality, it has a lowered second step and a lowered seventh step.
Pitch Names	The letter names associated with the sounds of pitches.

Preparatory Audiation	Hearing and comprehending music while in one of three "music babble" stages as a readiness for engaging in audiation.
Proper Names	The names of tonality classifications, tonal functions, meter classifications, and rhythm functions. For example, the classification of major and the function of tonic, and the classification of usual duple and the function of macro/microbeats.
Readiness	The necessary background to achieve a sequential objective.
Rest Pattern	One function of rhythm patterns. A rest pattern includes one or more rests. Macrobeats and microbeats are audiated during rests.
Resting Tone	Sometimes referred to as a "scale tone" or a "home tone." A tonal center or centers to which a piece of music gravitates. A resting tone is specified by a movable "do" syllable in the movable "do" system with a "la" based minor. A tonality has a resting tone, whereas a keyality has a tonic.
Rhythm	That which consists of three fundamental parts: macrobeats, microbeats, and rhythm patterns. In audiation, microbeats are superimposed on macrobeats, and melodic rhythm is superimposed on microbeats and macrobeats.
Rhythm Pattern	Two or more durations in a given meter that are audiated sequentially and form a whole.
Rhythm Solfege	See rhythm syllables.
Rhythm Syllables	Different names that are chanted for different durations in a rhythm pattern. The recommended rhythm syllables are based on

	beat functions rather than on the time-value names of notes.
Sonance	The overall audiation of two or more pitches sounding together, as in a chord.
Stabilized Music Aptitude	Music potential that is no longer affected by environmental factors. A child enters the stabilized music aptitude stage at approximately nine years old, and remains there.
Subdominant Pattern	One function of tonal patterns. In major tonality, for example, a subdominant pattern includes an arrangement of the tonal syllables "fa la do."
Subjective Keyality	A keyality for which there is no consensus.
Subjective Meter	A meter for which there is no consensus.
Subjective Tempo	A tempo for which there is no consensus.
Subjective Tonality	A tonality for which there is no consensus.
Subtonic	A pitch one half step below the leading tone, which is one whole step below the tonic (or resting tone). For example, if C is the tonic, the subtonic is Bb.
Syllable Names	Also called vocabulary names in learning sequence activities. For example, syllable names in a tonal pattern are "do so" and syllable names in a rhythm pattern are "du ta de ta."
Syntax	The orderly arrangement of pitches and durations that establishes the tonality and meter of a piece of music. Music has syntax but not grammar.
Tempo	1) The speed at which rhythm patterns are performed and 2) The relative lengths of macrobeats within rhythm patterns.

Tonal Pattern	Two, three, four, or five pitches in a given tonality that are audiated sequentially and form a whole. The eight pitches in a diatonic scale comprise at least two tonal patterns.
Tonal Solfege	See tonal syllables
Tonal Syllables	Different names that are sung for different pitches in a tonal pattern. The recommended tonal syllables are based on the movable "do" system with a "la" based minor, not a "do" based minor.
Tonality	That which is determined by the resting tone. If "do" is the resting tone, the tonality is major; if "la" is the resting tone, the tonality is harmonic minor or Aeolian; if "re" is the resting tone, the tonality is Dorian; if "mi" is the resting tone, the tonality is Phrygian; if "fa" is the resting tone, the tonality is Lydian; if "so" is the resting tone, the tonality is Mixolydian; and if "ti" is the resting tone, the tonality is Locrian. A tonality is always in a keyality but a keyality may not be in a tonality.
Tonic	The pitch name of a keyality. For example, C, D, or Eb. Keyality has a tonic, whereas a tonality has a resting tone.
Tonic Pattern	One function of tonal patterns. In major tonality, for example, it includes an arrangement of the tonal syllables "do mi so."
Triple Meter	See usual triple meter.
Unusual Meter	Four types of meter in which macrobeats are of unequal length, regardless of whether they are audiated in pairs or more than a pair, whether some of them are intact, or whether they are divided into two or three microbeats of equal length.

Upbeat Pattern	One function of rhythm patterns. An upbeat pattern occurs prior to the beginning of a macrobeat of a rhythm pattern and it becomes part of the rhythm pattern it precedes.
Usual Combined Meter	The meter that results when macrobeats of equal length are audiated in pairs. Some macrobeats are divided into two and others into three microbeats of unequal length.
Usual Duple Meter	The meter that results when macrobeats of equal length are audiated in pairs. Each macrobeat is divided into two microbeats of equal length.
Usual Meter	Three types of meter in which macrobeats of equal length are audiated in pairs. The macrobeats are divided into two or three microbeats of equal length or into two and three microbeats of unequal length, depending on the meter.
Usual Triple Meter	The meter that results when macrobeats of equal length are audiated in pairs. Each macrobeat is divided into three microbeats of equal length.

Index

A Music Learning Theory for Newborn and Young Children 8
Accents 16, 19
Advanced Measures of Music Audiation 93
Arpeggiated patterns (pitches moving by skips) 34
Audiation 2-6, 11
    13, 15, 16, 20
Aural perception 4

Blues 110
Body movement 6, 23, 34
    35, 68, 70, 95, 96

Chord symbols 12, 102
Chords 13, 64-91, 97, 98
Chromatics 99, 105, 118
Composition 1
Conductors 1, 2
Content/Context 9, 13
    16, 20, 65
Creativity 11

Diatonic patterns (pitches moving by steps) 34, 36
Dissonance 85, 90

Divisions 17, 19, 20, 25-32
Durations 20

Elongations 22, 25-32
Enrhythmic/enharmonic 34

Fingerings 117, 118
Fingers/gestures 102,103
    109, 110

Group instrumental instruction 117-119
Guidance 2

Harmonic improvisation   15
    65-103
Harmonic Improvisation Readiness Record and Rhythm Improvisation Readiness Record 9, 10, 63, 94, 96
Harmonic patterns 12, 13
    63, 64, 97, 98

Imitation . .2, 5, 13, 23-32, 36-42
Improvisation 1-9, 11-13
Individual differences 2, 6
    93-103
Instrumental improvisation   118
    119

Instrumental technique 117
*Intermediate Measures
   of Music Audiation* 93
*Introduction to Research and
   the Psychology of Music* 3
Inversions 115

Jazz 2, 5, 110

Keyality 65, 111

Language 3, 8, 9, 11, 13
*Learning Sequences in Music:
   Skill, Content, and Patterns* . .3
Listening 1

Macrobeats 15-22, 24-32
Major-minor seventh-chords
  98-103
Measure signature 17, 18-21
Melodic improvisation 15
Melodic patterns 12, 43-62
Melody 12, 13
Memorization 2, 6, 13
Memory 5
Meter 15-22, 24-32
   35-42, 43-62
Microbeats 15-22, 24-32
Minor-minor seventh-chords
  110-113
Mistakes/solutions 103
Modes 112
Modulations 98, 111
Music achievement . . .1, 2, 6, 11
Music aptitudes . .1, 2, 4, 6-8, 11
   Developmental/stabilized . . .7, 8

Musical background 3, 6, 7
Music education 2
Musical imagery 4
Music learning theory 12
Music theory 2, 13

Neutral syllables 24-32
   36-62, 99, 103
Non-harmonic tones . .46, 85-94
   101-105
Notation 2, 11, 13, 18

Popular music 110-113
*Preparatory Audiation, Audiation,
   and Music Learning Theory* . .3
Private lessons 7
Progressions 12 65-93, 105
Proper names 65

Range and tessitura 44
Rap performance 5
Readiness 7-9, 12, 15, 94-98
Reading 1, 11, 13
Recognition 5
Recorder 117-119
Research 9, 10
Resting tone 20, 33
Rests 16, 25, 28, 31
Rhythm 15-32
*Rhythm: Contrasting the
   Implications of Audiation
   and Notation* 16
Rhythm improvisation *23-32*
Rhythm patterns 12, 15-17
   20, 21, 43-65

INDEX

Rhythm syllables (solfege) .21, 22, 24-32, 43, 65, 99-103
Roots 66, 99

Scat singing 5
Schelling, Felix Emanuel 7
Sequential learning 8, 9, 15
Studies in Harmonic and Rhythmic Improvisation ..9, 96

Teaching/learning 8, 9
Tempo 16, 24
Tonal improvisation ...15, 34-42
Tonal patterns 12, 33-43, 65
Tonal syllables (solfege) ...33-43, 65, 99-103
Tonality 33-41, 43-62
Tonic 33, 34
Transposition 44

Underlying macrobeats ...23-32

Variation 12
Vocabularies 12